INTERIM MINISTRY

Positive Change in Times of Transition

Dr. Justin W. Tull

Copyright 2012

Interim Ministry: Positive Change in Times of Transition
Copyright 2012 ©Justin W Tull
All rights Reserved

No part of this book may be reproduced or transmitted in any form or by any means, electronic or mechanical, including photocopying and recording or by any information storage or retrieval system.

Cover photo by Larry Phillips.
Cover and interior design by Sidewalk Labs.

Requests for permission should be addressed to justinwtull@yahoo.com

ISBN: 1479335959
ISBN-13: 978-1479335954

Scripture Quotations, unless otherwise indicated, are from New Revised Standard Version Bible, Copyright 1989
National Council of the Churches of Christ in the United States of America.
Used by permission. All rights reserved.

CONTENTS

INTRODUCTION 1

FIRST INTERIM 5
STAGE ONE: *FROM CHAOS AND DESPAIR TO ORDER & HOPE* 5
  THE CALL TO INTERIM MINISTRY 5
  FIRST MEETINGS 7
  THE LAY OF THE LAND 9
    Devastating Grief
    Financial Disaster
    Leadership Void
    Crisis of Identity
    No Plan for the Future
  IMMEDIATE GOALS 11
    Deal with Grief
    Instill Hope in the Church's Financial Future
    Encourage the Staff
    Preach to the Situation at Hand; Then Preach the Basics
    Meet with the People
    Strengthen Pastoral Care
    Assume Leadership
  INITIAL COMMUNICATION 15
    INSERT: *First Letter to Church Members* 16
    INSERT: *First Pastoral Reflection* 19
  WORSHIP DECISIONS AND GOALS 21
    INSERT: *First Sermon: "A Light in Darkness"* 13
  MONEY MATTERS 28
    Providing Leadership to Finance Committee
    Philosophy of Church Giving
    Avoid the Sinking Ship Syndrome
    New Hope for Finances
  STATE OF THE CHURCH AFTER ONE MONTH 30
STAGE TWO: GETTING IT TOGETHER 32
  POSITIVE SIGNS 32
  WHO ARE WE? IN SEARCH OF OUR IDENTITY 33
    INSERT: Pastoral Reflection: *Becoming Balcony People* 35
  STAFF ISSUES 40

INSERT: *Posting the Colors*	42
CRUCIAL ISSUES	45
STAGE THREE: MOVING INTO THE FUTURE	**48**
STEPS TOWARDS TRANSITION	48
POSITIVE SIGNS OF VITALITY	50
Easter Worship	
INSERT: Reflections: *Signs of Easter!*	51
New Member Sunday	
Celebration of the New Building	
Confirmation for the Youth	
STEWARDSHIP EMPHASIS	54
INSERT: *Extra-Mile Giving Letter*	55
PHASING OUT MY LEADERSHIP	57
FINAL WORDS	57
Last Sermons	
INSERT: *Goodbye and Thank You!* (Final Letter)	59
SECOND INTERIM	**61**
PHASE I: FROM HIGH ANXIETY TO IMPROVED MORALE	**61**
INITIAL ENCOUNTERS	61
INITIAL OBSERVATION: TOTAL MELTDOWN	63
INITIAL STRATEGY	64
DIAGNOSTIC GOALS	65
DIAGNOSING THE MELTDOWN	67
Appointive Process Issues	
Vision Confusion	
Identity Versus Vision	
Failure to Grow	
Disenfranchisement	
ADDRESSING THE ISSUES	72
Preaching Plan	
INSERT: *First Letter to the Congregation*	74
Pastoral Reflection: *Gtah @Our Church*	77
STATE OF THE CHURCH	79
PHASE II: *STABILIZATION AND RENEWED HOPE*	**81**
MEANINGFUL WORSHIP: A KEY TO RECOVERY	81
Early Worship Changes	

    Worship Survey
    Decision Making Process for Cutting a Service
    Reflction: *Discerning Our Worship Identity*   85
    Lenten Plan
    Preaching Plan
  REFLECTIONS   89
  GETTING OUR HOUSE IN ORDER   90
    New Member Sunday
    Supporting Mission Identity
    Transformation Decision
  STEWARDSHIP WORK   92
    Personal Example
    Educating the Finance Committee
    Letters to New Members about Giving
    INSERT: *Stewardship Letter: Extra-Mile Giving*   95
  State of the Church: Cautious Optimism   97
PHASE III: *PREPARING FOR THE FUTURE*   99
  FINAL STEPS   99
    Staff Renewal
    Final Worship Decision
    Sunday School and Small Groups
    New Member Sunday
    Preparing for a New Senior Pastor
  PREACHING PLAN   102
  PASTORAL REFLECTIONS   103
  STATE OF THE CHURCH   104
    INSERT: *Looking Backward, Looking Forward (Final Reflection)*   106

EPILOGUE: HEALTH OF CHURCHES AFTER INTERIM   109

REFLECTIONS ON INTERIM MINISTRY   111

ROLE OF PREACHING IN INTERIM MINISTRY   115

KEYS TO EFFECTIVE INTERIM MINISTRY   119

INTRODUCTION

Interim Ministry: Positive Change in Times of Transition is an attempt to share in-depth case studies of my first two interim appointments. It goes well beyond offering simply theories and methodologies of how to do interim ministry. Instead it details concrete examples of how the initial goals of the interim pastor may be implemented through programs, group interaction, pastoral care, sermons, and written communication. Perhaps equally important to taking on the various issues is knowing when to move to the next stage of the transition. (This is especially important when dealing with the issue of congregational grief.) An interim minister must be skilled in being able to read the lay of the land, both in times of chaos and in subsequent times of initial healing and growth.

Both of these interim appointments were six months or less in length and both churches were experiencing significant crisis and high anxiety. Even so, I believe the analytical skills, goal-setting, and concrete strategies used in these two appointments are readily transferable to longer tenured and less chaotic interim experiences. Care has been taken in the sharing of these two interim experiences to list in a concise way the major dynamics of each church's story. Though no effort has been made to disguise the identity of these two churches, I have omitted the names of the churches as well as persons involved in the unfolding stories.

During my initial interim experience, I discovered two major surprises. First, I was astonished that in the midst of chaos and high anxiety that so many positive changes could take place, changes in many cases unrelated to the major sources of the crisis situation. In both cases significant improvements were made in finances, church identity, vision, theological understanding, lay leadership, and general church morale. Second, I soon discovered in my first appointment, and later re-confirmed it in my second, that even when there has been a clearly defined source of the crisis, e.g. grief from the death of a pastor, or a problem of ministerial leadership, there also proved to be a multiplicity of other issues that desperately needed to be addressed—often things like lay leadership, staff conflict, church identity, and unresolved issues of the past. What is most promising about interim ministry is that in the midst of transition and even chaos, the church is often more open to change than in times of status quo. Indeed, both of the churches I served made tremendous strides in becoming much healthier churches—all within the short tenure of my time with them.

I have purposely shared in depth both my strategy and goals for these two churches as well as many of the

Introduction

concrete ways I tried to fulfill them. I have included individual goals and in many cases offered documents that were part of my implementation—outlines of programs, letters to the congregation, pastoral reflections, and sermon plans. I have offered these as concrete examples of ways the interim minister can provide leadership for positive change in the midst of transition.

As a result of my two interim experiences, coupled with significant training in interim ministry, I have become a huge fan of interim ministry as a way of offering skilled and trained leadership to churches in the midst of transition—whether that be a time after a death in the pastoral family, following ministerial malfeasance, during an illness of the current pastor, or following a long pastorate. Interim ministry, in my view, should never be seen as a period for "marking time." At its best it should always foster positive change even in difficult times.

I hope that the stories of these two interim appointments will be beneficial to all seeking a fuller understanding of the specific role of interim ministry. Though these two interim appointments have demonstrated positive results—both during my ministry there and since—I do not claim that the positive results are simply a product of effective strategies or my own gifts and graces, but neither do I short-change the huge role effective leadership can play in such crisis situations. The strategies employed in such situations coupled with the theology, faith and integrity of the senior interim pastor are indeed crucial in the transformation of churches from a crisis mode to one of hope and vitality. Equally, if not more important, to the success of interim ministry are the workings of the Holy

Spirit and the willingness of members of the congregation to heal, dream new visions, and commit themselves to a new level of discipleship.

    I hope that the concrete details of these two interim appointments will be a catalyst for individual reflection and professional dialogue as numerous interim ministers begin their own work as transformational agents. I trust they will lead the church toward a more hopeful and fruitful future.

FIRST INTERIM

STAGE ONE: *FROM CHAOS AND DESPAIR TO ORDER & HOPE*

THE CALL TO INTERIM MINISTRY

I received the call the day before Thanksgiving asking if I would come out of retirement to serve as interim senior pastor of a church in crisis. Since I was aware of this particular church and its situation I immediately knew that this would be a most challenging task. Twice in my ministry I had been appointed to churches in the midst of a crisis. The first was to follow a person who left the church abruptly to file for divorce and leave ministry. The second crisis was following the unexpected death of a beloved pastor who died suddenly just before Christmas. My initial thought when I was asked to become the interim pastor of a church whose young minister was near death after a long battle with cancer was that this appointment would be more difficult than either of my former challenging appointments.

But the compelling reason I felt strongly a sense of call to this particular church was my own recent experience with tragedy. Years earlier my wife, age 56, was diagnosed with a malignant brain tumor and died 27 months later. Because of this experience and my insights into how her illness and death had affected the church, I knew I had a personal understanding of what this new church had been facing and what might lie ahead. In addition, I had written a book on the issue of facing tragedy some eight years before my own faith would be tested by my wife's illness. After prayerful consideration and discussion with my new wife, Janette, I called my District Superintendent to say, "Yes."

Monday morning I made plans to meet on Thursday with the pastor who was in the final stages of her life. We were to talk about the transition from her leadership to mine. On Tuesday morning, however, I received a call that she had just died. On Wednesday I met with her husband and his parents. That night I met with the Staff Parish Relations Committee. Saturday I attended the pastor's beautiful memorial service with two thousand people present. That Sunday I would preach three worship services to a congregation still in shock and deep grief. That first week was filled with intense emotion, deep faith, and poignant intimacy. My interim journey had begun in the midst of chaos.

FIRST MEETINGS

❖ Staff Parish Relations Committee

I met with the staff parish committee to talk about their needs and to offer my thoughts and my support. I shared the story of my wife's illness and death and the insights I had gained from that experience. I wanted them to know that I understood in part their journey. I knew both the burden and the blessing of being a witness to someone dying in the midst of the church community. I listened to them share concern about the morale of the youth, the possible negative effect of this death upon the children, and the future of the church. We talked about the trouble with church finances, the exhaustion of the staff, and of the need for leadership in several sectors.

I left the meeting impressed with the courage and caliber of the committee and heartened by their vote of confidence in my coming. I thought that if the rest of the church was like this group, then it would be a privilege to serve in their midst even under such difficult circumstances.

I asked for only one commitment from the group. I wanted their assurance that we would not reduce our staff even with the church's finances in bad shape. I wanted to be able to tell the staff when I met with them that their jobs were secure. I would need all of their efforts in order to meet the needs of a hurting congregation. The committee gave me their promise to keep the staff intact.

❖ Staff Meeting

My first meeting with the staff was filled with emotion and some heavy anxiety. I was glad to tell them that their jobs were secure. I shared with them my life story as I had with Staff Parish and asked them to share with me their thoughts and feelings in the face of their pastor's death. I assured them that I would be taking major leadership responsibility but that I had no interest and certainly no time to micromanage the staff. I urged them to begin their grief work, to get help if need be, and to take some time off as they could. Most importantly, I suggested that we as a staff needed to heal first in order to help the congregation to heal. If we remained wounded and broken, the congregation would not be encouraged to move on. I assured them that I was always open for them to share feelings and issues related to their pastor's illness, death, and style of ministry. This was to be one safe place to work on grief and to raise issues related to this larger-than-life minister.

❖ Meeting the Deceased's Family

The initial response of the family was warm and gracious though it was only two days after the minister's death. I offered to the widower and his parents my pastoral support. I suggested to the clergy spouse that I might be not only his pastor but also a friend since I had indeed taken the journey he was about to make. Through the next few months, I continued to reach out to him to offer guidance and pastoral care. He would eventually make the decision to leave the church his wife had served though he left his young son in the church's creative school until the end of the semester. His sister and their parents would also decide later to leave the church. The parents of the deceased, though it was painful for them, stayed at the church throughout my six-month interim. Later when they found being in worship too painful, they continued to volunteer to help at the church on Wednesdays. In such situations as these the dynamic of the deceased's family has great potential to become problematic or even divisive. I was most grateful that the actions and attitudes of the deceased's family did not seem to negatively impact the church's recovery.

THE LAY OF THE LAND

It was soon obvious to me that this church was facing many serious problems at the same time it was dealing with deep grief. The congregation was in shock—not without hope—but with no real confidence as to how they could recover. Listed below are the key problems I readily identified:

- **Devastating Grief**

Anyone who was active in the church was painfully aware of the awful signs of their pastor's illness. There were times she had to sit rather than stand; times she fainted, times when she was not as mentally alert as usual. And her body was the ultimate sign of her formidable illness, thin and weak. The more the people loved her, the more tragic and unfair her illness became. Her death was the ultimate injustice. How could one so loving, so compassionate, suffer such a fate?

- **Financial Disaster**

For several years the unspoken financial plan had worked: budget planning based on projecting a 15% growth in giving each year. (This had been possible because of the rapid grow of membership.) Unfortunately several things

First Interim

happened at once to foil that plan. The first was the pastor's illness which certainly had some adverse effect even with her valiant efforts. The second was a recent increase in the budget due to staff expansion coupled with a new building program. If that were not enough, then came the downturn in the economy. By the time I arrived in December, all the major bills had been paid except for debt retirement, but only by "borrowing" from designated funds. By the end of December, we were in debt to ourselves by about $50,000 and had no reserves left. We would start the New Year with no reserve money at all for cash flow.

❖ **Leadership Void**

There was also a crisis in leadership. Several areas had been left without any pastoral oversight—finance being one of them. Pastoral care was also under strain because the associate, already over-stretched by trying to hold things together, could not meet all the pastoral care needs of the congregation. She was exhausted although she continued valiantly trying to keep as many balls in the air as possible. Many small groups within the church had not been receiving pastoral support or attention. This void was not the fault of anyone—neither the staff nor the congregation. It was simply a result of having a senior pastor who could no longer carry a full load because of a very debilitating illness.

❖ **Crisis of Identity**

The church was also suffering from a crisis of identity. Many of the church saw their charismatic leader as the true secret to the church's vitality and identity. When they experienced her death, they thought that the church's future was indeed severely threatened. Many also saw the church's identity as being completely shaped by her personality, theology and passion. They failed to realize that though she had helped shape part of the church's identity, it had long since taken on a life of its own. During my interim a wise church consultant would provide a wonderfully insightful analogy: "The church has its own DNA; the pastor simply puts his or her fingerprints on it."

❖ No Plan for the Future

Just as there was a leadership void at the church, the church was also void of any clear vision. There was a new building under construction, but no obvious plan for expansion of church programming or ministry. Since the church had been in a "survival mode" during their pastor's illness, it had had scarce opportunity to look toward the future—simply "hanging in" was the order of the day. There was little room for vision in the midst of chaos. Coping was the mode, not envisioning.

IMMEDIATE GOALS

In the face of these problems, I formulated almost immediately several initial goals for my interim ministry. Most of these need only a little embellishment.

❖ Deal with Grief

I preached at this church what I always preached in the face of crisis and tragedy—hope in God's presence and power. I wanted to reassure the congregation that God was with them and they would be all right. I had a unique perspective because I had experienced such presence and power in my own struggles with my wife's illness and subsequent death. I could preach such hope not only because I believed it, but also because I had truly experienced it as a gift.

❖ Instill Hope in the Church's Financial Future

From the very beginning, I never viewed the financial crisis as one caused by a tanking economy. I thought it was primarily a result of poor stewardship. One of my goals was for the budget to be in the black when I passed the baton to the next senior pastor. I would begin sharing my stewardship rationale with the Finance committee and work outward. I would avoid the image at all costs that the church was a "sinking ship." No one wants to contribute to a hopeless cause.

❖ Encourage the Staff

Though I sensed that the staff had been more burdened by their pastor's illness and subsequent death than had the congregation at large, I knew it was crucial for the staff do their grieving as soon as possible and move on. If the staff remained wounded and depressed it would hinder the healing of the congregation as a whole. I also knew they needed physical rest in order to recover. I asked all of them to take time off as they were able. In the weeks that followed I would carefully monitor their recovery and express concern for their well being.

❖ Preach to the Situation at Hand; Then Preach the Basics

At the first of my ministry at the church, I met head on the issues that the congregation faced: grief, questions of faith, renewal of hope, and compassion for each other. After a month, however, I moved on to preach some of the basics of the faith: prayer, salvation, the role of ministry and the church, stewardship, and our common call to ministry. The nature and progression of my preaching reflected what I thought to be the proper timeline for the grieving process.

❖ Meet with the People

I have never liked to "flit around" in the congregation, just making small talk and greeting people. But during my interim I was very intentional about visiting with people before the service because I knew that they were in need of human warmth. I was amazed at how many times the conversation skipped the small talk altogether and went straight to substantive matters.

I also was very intentional about visiting with small groups in the church: United Methodist Men, United Methodist Women, retired men's lunch group, and the senior citizen's group. I was also very faithful to attend fund raisers, youth events, and children's programs. My presence at these "optional events" (My appointment was "half-time") was a witness to the congregation that I was not a "short-timer" but one who had thoroughly attached myself to them. It was not just "their" church; it was "my" church as well.

❖ Strengthen Pastoral Care

One of my earliest goals was to involve myself substantially in pastoral care. One benefit would be to give some relief to the associate who had been carrying too much of the load. But more importantly, I would be involved with the lives of people who had real spiritual needs. My presence in the hospitals and homes also gave me credibility as a minister who not only preached but also cared.

❖ Assume Leadership

I decided upon arrival that I would need to be involved in several key committees where the senior pastor had not been involved. Both Finance and Trustees would receive my attendance and leadership in the next few months. What surprised me was that my leadership was affirmed and respected in every aspect of the church life. I was amazed at how open people were to my insights and suggestions. I have never felt so respected for my experience and knowledge of church matters. Church leaders seemed quite ready for someone to give them some direction without dictating all the details or outcome. I was spending much time listening to them. They were now returning the favor.

INITIAL COMMUNICATION

❖ First Letter to Church Members

During my third week I sent out a letter (Text to follow) that attempted to do the following:

(The sentences in parentheses give the unspoken message I was trying to convey.)

- Acknowledge the loss of a great pastor. (*We have a reason to be hurting.*)
- Introduce myself to the congregation. (*We now have a new leader to help us.*)
- State that the church is at an important crossroads. (*We all need to pull together.*)
- Lift the inspiring example of the children of the church raising money by selling lemonade for the church budget. (*If the kids care enough about the church to give, why not us?*)
- Inform the congregation that the Finance committee had renegotiated lower loan payments and lowered next year's budget. (*We are being frugal and realistic with the money that has been given.*)
- Tell them that my salary lowered expenses by $40,000 over the previous senior pastor's salary. (*We now have $40,000 more dollars than before.*)
- Inform them that I would be tithing my salary to the church. (*I am setting an example and showing my commitment to "our" church.*)
- End with an affirmation of all the good things that were happening at the church. (*People support a church that matters to them.*)

First Interim

Dear Church Family,

    I am honored to serve as Interim senior pastor of this church. You have a talented and dedicated staff, gifted lay leadership who understand the mission and ministry of the church, and a caring congregation. Though I know and understand something of the enormity of your grief with the loss of such a beloved pastor, I also sense the resiliency of your faith and your commitment to the future of the church. Such faith and commitment are due in part to the witness of your beloved minister's ministry, the workings of the Holy Spirit, and the loving support of staff and fellow members.

    Today we stand at a crossroads in the life of the church. Many challenges stand before us. Many opportunities await us. As the church building is being re-shaped and re-formed, our church life and mission await our decision to move forward boldly into the future.

    Last Sunday I was privileged to witness the children of our church bringing forward their gifts to help with the church budget. Led by the vision of a young girl, our children raised over $875 selling lemonade over several weeks to supportive church members. The church obviously matters to these children. They heard about a financial need. They acted. We as adults should be both proud of their actions and strongly encouraged to do something ourselves.

    Over the past several months, the leadership of the church has worked hard to meet the financial challenge of this time. They have been determined to retain our dedicated staff. Certainly my coming on board as half-time interim pastor was one way to free up money for other uses. As a part of my commitment to this church, I will give a tithe of my salary to the annual budget. I will also strive to use all my gifts and leadership to ensure that the church moves forward and continues to meet both the needs of this congregation as well as serve the larger community.

You will be delighted to know that our lending institution has been sensitive to our needs and has worked to reconstruct our debt retirement. This will mean the church's financial needs are now within the reach of this congregation even in the midst of tough economic times – but not without the strong support of our church members.

I hope you perceive as I do that this church has a great future, a future worth investing in. Since coming to this church, I have seen numerous signs of vitality and faithfulness: some of the sharpest laity I have ever met, a great staff with both exceptional gifts and deep devotion to ministry, vibrant programs for youth and children, outstanding worship and music, compassion and warmth in the hearts of so many church members, and a contagious commitment to mission around the globe. These are all a vibrant part of who we are. As we begin a new year and a new chapter in the life of our church, these characteristics will need to be reaffirmed as our on-going identity as a church.

I look forward to greeting you in worship in the weeks ahead and becoming an intimate part of this church family.

Grace and Peace, Justin

First Interim

❖ **First Pastoral Reflection**

In my first reflection I tried to mirror back to the congregation how I saw them as a church. This would be their first step in re-thinking their church identity. I also wanted to lift up to a grieving congregation some of their strengths, encourage them to show compassion to each other, and to begin to offer my pastoral support. (The text of the reflection follows.)

No one has ever accused me of being intuitive, psychic, or even especially observant. I don't even notice body language unless it is extreme. My strengths are being systematic, analytical, theological—all with a practical twist. But even with my weakness of observation, I have picked up on several things since I came your way only a month ago.

In my first column to you, I want to share three brief observations about the ministries of the church – one without reproach, one with a great start but room to grow, and one that I see as a growing edge for the church.

The most impressive thing about this church is its high commitment to mission, especially foreign mission. Certainly that strength was given momentum and emphasis by your devoted pastor's passion for missions. But now, I believe, the church has reached a point of no return: you could never revert back to just being a church concerned about itself. Too many people have felt the joy and meaning that comes when one reaches out beyond oneself and one's comfort zone. This church will always be a church committed to missions and that exercise in Christian compassion will help make a difference to others while helping it grow as the body of Christ.

Second, there is a high level of caring and intimacy among the members of this church. I felt that intimacy when I met with your church leadership before being appointed to the church. I experienced that intimacy through eye contact while serving Holy Communion my first Sunday. I have witnessed such caring in the interaction between church members and staff. But I also know that all people do not receive such special notice or welcome at the church. I have had a few friends of mine visit the

First Interim

church who were barely noticed and certainly not welcomed. Hospitality to strangers has to be intentional or it will be limited to a warm welcome just among friends – and that is not true hospitality. I see this church as having a great start toward genuine hospitality because we already practice it. What remains is to expand our hospitality to include all people.

The third area is one that requires considerable growth if this church is to be a vital church – not only in its mission beyond its borders, but in its direct ministry to the community. This critical area for growth is stewardship. First, let me assure you that I don't know what anyone in this church makes or how much anyone gives. But I have served enough churches to know that we are not doing all we can to support our ministries. This church should never be content with just a bare bones budget for staff and the on-going ministries. We should have enough financial support from our members that we have the luxury of being imaginative about what new ministries we can begin with the money available. Even in these tough economic times, the church should be giving at a level that would lift us out of a survival mode and into a healthy growth mode. This, of course, will only happen when the congregation decides to make the church a high priority in their spending. I hope I will see this happen before I leave next May. It is one of my goals.

It remains an honor to serve you and with you at this transitional time in the life of our church. You are a great church. I look forward to seeing you become even better. If you have a pastoral need, please be sure to call so that we can minister to you.   Grace and Peace, Justin Tull

WORSHIP DECISIONS AND GOALS

❖ Service Planning

When I began my interim I thought I would put my personal design on the worship service—make a few changes so that it would be easier for the next pastor to make further changes. I soon decided to leave the associate and music director in charge of designing the service and opt for following the established worshipping tradition. It was perhaps the best decision I made as to what *not* to do. I believe in retrospect that the familiarity of the worship order helped people find a comfort level for their grieving. It also helped the people make the transition to new leadership in worship.

I did take on one task I had not previously planned to do—doing the children's sermon almost every week. This was due in part to the polite but firm resistance of the staff to take that responsibility and also my concern that the children have some continuity from Sunday to Sunday. It was a decision that reaped a great reward and perhaps my best compliment. After one worship service I received a note and drawing from a young girl that said, *"Great sermon! You rock!"*

❖ First Sermon

In my first sermon preached the second Sunday in Advent I shared my own tragic story of loss and grief and thus became one with them. I understood their difficult journey and I empathized with them. But I was also clear to stress that I was not defeated by my own tragedy—not because I was strong—but because God had indeed empowered me to let go of my sorrow and move forward as

First Interim

a more compassionate creature. I tried to assure the congregation that the journey they had already travelled was not just filled with heavy sadness, but also laden with intimacy and meaning. They had my full empathy and compassion—but not my pity. They had shared the witness of a wonderful, gifted, compassionate minister who suffered an early death but who was never defeated by either her illness or her death. The pain of her loss should never wipe out the tremendous gain of having experienced her loving presence for so many years. The power of her witness must continue to inspire and not be lost by her death.

A LIGHT IN DARKNESS
Sermon Excerpts

Today is a sad day in the life of this church and the larger community. You have lost a most gifted and caring pastor. Her family has lost a loving wife and a devoted mother. Nothing can take away our sense of loss or the tragic nature of what has happened.

Those who were at her memorial service yesterday have already celebrated her life among us. Many of you were able to say goodbye before she died, to feel her embrace and to witness her amazing strength and faith. But now we must deal with the void that her death has brought to us. We may have faced the reality of her death but we have only begun to grieve our loss. We yearn to have a faith like hers, a faith that was deep and wise.

Today as we gather as a church family we are sad, but we still gather to pray, to sing, and to give thanks to God, and to embrace one another in love and compassion. We also gather in the hope of hearing God's word to us and feeling the comfort of God's presence.

I come to you today as a stranger, yet as one of you, for I share your faith. I share your love and respect for your departed pastor. I also come as one who knows something of your pain. I know at least what it feels like to lose someone you love, someone who not only lives well but dies well, someone who dies before her time.

Before I become a part of your story, I would like to

share something of my story, my faith journey, especially the last 13 years. In 1995 I published a book of sermons entitled Why God Why? Like Kushner's book, *When Bad Things Happen to Good People*, I addressed the problem of human tragedy and sought to offer Faith's response. I did not do so out of my own tragic circumstances—my family had not yet faced a major tragedy. I spoke instead out of my experience of pastoring countless families who had endured so many tragedies—untimely deaths, betrayals, undeserved suffering, destructive criticism. These experiences had caused many of them to cry out," Why, God, Why? Why did you allow these things to happen?"

Then on September 25, 2001, only weeks after the horrors of 9/11 my family experienced a devastating blow: my 56-year-old wife was diagnosed with terminal brain cancer. Two days later she had brain surgery – one that left her with brain function but eventually led to a wheelchair due to a weakened left side of her body. Though she was only expected to live for three months, she lived 27 months and received her deepest wish, to see the birth of her first grandchild.

The next two years were filled with chemo and recovery, setbacks and encouragement. I was the night-time care giver for those two years. It was difficult but I was able to keep my promise to sleep beside her each night. But I would not have been able to care for my wife without the love and support of the church staff and my congregation. When I realized that I could not work full-time, I went before the Staff Parish Relations Committee and I told them I could only work about 75% of my normal work load. I told them how I planned to divide responsibilities among the staff and that we had already planned out the next two months. But I did not know if they would accept my limited ministry. I knew they might want to make plans for a change of pastor.

After hearing my proposal they asked for some time to discuss the matter. A short time later they called me back into the room. I was anxious. I thought they might want me to go on leave of absence.

"We have only one problem," they said.

"What is that?" I asked.

"We are afraid you will work too much. We want your permission to be able to tell you when we think you are working too much!"

This was the greatest gift the church could have given to me and to Lynn. They wanted me to not only minister to them but also to minister to one they had grown to love.

During those two years there were times that the church suffered some from my limited time and energy. But I preached almost every Sunday. And I can guarantee you that I did not preach a shallow sermon during that time. There was a poignancy that grounded every sermon. It was some of my best preaching I have ever done because I did it in the very face of death.

I believe the church is a stronger church now because it decided to minister to me and to my family. It was able to look sickness and death in the face and know that ultimately neither is to be feared. It experienced the intimacy of caring for people who are suffering and coming to believe that the Christian faith has something to offer to every situation even the most tragic.

My wife, Lynn, was incredible in the midst of her illness and in the face of death. Never once did she feel self pity. Never once did she focus on dying, only living. She was in church and in the choir almost every Sunday until the last few months before her death. She was a great witness to her faith just as your beloved pastor has been.

A friend of mine spoke to me one day with a timid voice, "Can I ask you a very personal question?"

I said, "Sure."

"Has Lynn's illness shaken your faith?"

"Absolutely not," I said.

"Her illness has shaken me to the core, but not my faith."

My theology has always been one that expected suffering. I never thought I would be exempt from hardship or tragedy. The words of William Sloan Coffin are perhaps the most profound way of stating my theology. Rev. Coffin lost his young adult son in a tragic automobile accident. Two weeks later he would have to preach. He told his congregation in the sermon, "I believe in a God of minimum protection and maximum support." (Credo, William Sloane Coffin, p. 10)

That is what I experienced throughout those 27 months of my wife's illness and the grief that followed her death. I felt maximum support—support from my church, my family, and from God. There were times that I felt I had no more resources inside me. Unless I received power from beyond myself, I did not think I could keep going. That power to endure always came to me. I experienced it as a gift.

From Chaos and Despair to Order and Hope

I now know something of the elements of human tragedy—seeing someone I love, someone with so much left to give, have her life cut short and our life together come to an end. But personal experience with tragedy is not the main reason I feel called to be your pastor. I am not here simply because I know something of what you have gone through and much of what you will go through in the coming weeks and months. I am here because I believe that our faith is stronger than tragedy. I am here because I can offer to you a message of hope. I am here because I believe what Paul came to believe.

Do you remember the words God spoke to Paul in our Scripture for today? As Paul prayed to God for release from pain and suffering God offered to him words of assurance: "My Grace is sufficient for you" (2 Corinthians 12:9).

Many years ago I offered such words of hope to a grieving congregation, one that had lost nine beloved members during the Advent season. Later those same words would become the last words of my book on facing human tragedy. I believe they have a word for you—not holly jolly words, not sugar-coated words, but words that offer hope in the midst of grief.

There is still crying in Bethlehem and Ramah. Good people become ill. The saints still die. But the Christ Child still comes. The light still shines. And the darkness will never, never, never overcome it. Thanks be to God!

(Why God, Why? Sermons on the Problem of Pain, p. 103)

First Interim

❖ Subsequent Sermons

The remaining sermons in December moved to more indirect references to the tragedy that had shaken the church to its core. By the third message I injected a bit of humor and lifted up other people who suffered drastic human needs—the poor, the neglected, the hurting. (Focusing on the pain of others can draw us out of self pity and self absorption. Indeed, many suffer more than we do.)

In January, I would have to address a theological question that was beginning to surface within the congregation: "How could God allow our pastor to die when we prayed in faith for her to live? Where was our miracle?" My sermon was entitled: "Prayer: Beyond a Genie Mentality!" It suggested that prayer does not simply grant us all our desires, no matter how heart-felt or magnanimous. Prayer is intended as a relationship, not as a request line.

MONEY MATTERS

❖ Providing Leadership to Finance Committee

My first meeting with finance was strategically important. First, I wanted to make clear that their function was not to simply control the purse strings so that expenditures were totally dependent on income. Rather, their first objective was to help the church reach the budget that would enable much-needed ministries. Having said that, I acknowledged that in times of crisis some cut backs are necessary. I assured them that the staff would use restraint in spending any of their budgeted funds. But I also insisted that now was not the time to cut staff. We needed the staff intact to get the church back on its feet. I even suggested that we put back in the budget $15,000 for a communications person, so essential to keep the church body informed. (In January they would vote to keep that position and it was then approved by the Administrative Board.) This was quite a leap of faith for a church fearful of bankruptcy.

❖ Philosophy of Church Giving

In that first meeting I also shared with them my philosophy of church giving. It is a very simple formula that had proven true in all the churches I had served. The thesis is this: "If the congregation is healthy, the financial goal reachable, and the congregation is informed on a regular basis of the financial situation, then the financial goal will be reached or come very close to it." From my observation, the church, despite its grief, was a very healthy church; the financial goal was well within its reach given the affluence of the congregation. However, I was suspicious that the church was not fully aware of the extent of the financial problems until the finances were on the brink of disaster. One of the things they needed to do better, I thought, was to give people a true picture of the state of the church, not just in dollars and cents, but also in the value of its life and ministries.

❖ Avoid the Sinking Ship Syndrome

I told the finance committee that I wanted to stop the impression that their church was a "sinking ship"—stop simply emphasizing the seriousness of the situation with little motivation except to say it was an emergency. I had learned that shortly before I arrived that a letter had been sent to the congregation stating that the staff would have to be reduced if giving did not increase. This was done as the senior pastor was in the last stages of her life. I was not openly critical of that move given the grave circumstances, but I told them we now needed a different strategy. I wanted to motivate the congregation to give because of the great things that were being done and to give them hope that we could once again reach our goal.

❖ New Hope for Finances

After sharing my philosophy, I asked that they join the Staff Parish Relations Committee by committing to keep the present staff even though we were behind on meeting the budget. I reminded them that my salary would provide a $40,000 savings from the previous senior pastor's salary. They were also aware of other promising developments. Key church leaders had already begun to meet with the holder of our mortgage requesting a change in our payment plan for the next year. (Later the lender would agree to restructure our loan payment temporarily to give us much-needed breathing room—a savings of almost $100,000 from the previous year's budget.) I left the Finance meeting feeling that they were now starting to see a glimmer of hope and seemed open to my leadership in trying to strengthen church giving.

STATE OF THE CHURCH AFTER ONE MONTH

By the end of December, I was very pleased with the progress that had been made. My assessment was that many were well on their way in grieving the loss of a beloved pastor. One indicator was that the Christmas Eve service did not seem to be an overly emotional experience for the worshippers as I had expected. I am certain that all who attended thought of the recently deceased pastor and were aware of her absence, but there were few signs of people being overly emotional or devastated even at such a poignant time. I was convinced that the congregation was on its way to being healed.

In general, the church seemed to be reaching a new sense of normalcy. There was a growing confidence that they were going to be all right, that they would make it. The staff was beginning to recover from fatigue and morale seemed to be improving. The giving at the end of the year was good but not enough to repay funds we had borrowed from ourselves to pay all the current bills. We would begin the New Year with a significant debt to ourselves, no bills, and no reserve funds.

STAGE TWO: GETTING IT TOGETHER
POSITIVE SIGNS

❖ **Finances and Attendance Show Growth**

By the end of January, the church had something to celebrate: attendance was slightly up from the previous year and giving was more than $60,000 over the previous January, leaving us with a reserve of $8,888 to begin February.

❖ **Why God Why? Seminar Addresses Grief Issue**

Early on, I decided that a seminar on my book, *Why, God, Why?* might be helpful with those having trouble dealing with their pastor's death, especially those for whom it was a crisis of faith. I offered a 4-session course that met on Tuesday evenings. Later, at the request from the group, I extended it for two more weeks. The big surprise was that the group did not spend most of the discussion time talking about issues surrounding their pastor's illness and death.

Instead they brought up their own tragedies that had raised for them questions of faith: the loss of a child, the death of a young adult brother, a prolonged illness, job loss, unanswered prayer.

The other surprise was that the group included several non-members and many who had not been that active in the church. Subsequently, one member of the group joined the church and several others became more active.

Though it was awkward at times talking about intimate and personal matters in a group of ten to twenty-two people, the seminar did provide an important time of theological reflection and perhaps even theological formation. The fact that the group asked to continue for extra sessions is a testimony to its meaning, at least for the final group of eleven.

WHO ARE WE? IN SEARCH OF OUR IDENTITY

❖ **United Methodist Men**

When I attended my first United Methodist Men's meeting in early January, I was surprised to find myself as the total center of attention. I quickly turned to the group of twenty-two men to see if I could begin to understand more of the church's uniqueness. The group was composed of men who had become members under the two senior pastors: the founding pastor and the pastor who had recently died. Both ministers had experienced very effective ministries but were markedly different in style, personality, and philosophy of the church.

I asked the group to share with me what drew them to this particular church. Why did they join and what was still important to them about their church? The astounding feedback from the group was an almost unanimous consensus. All who were there, from charter member to a recent church visitor, spoke of the sense of closeness, the caring community, the intimacy that they had experienced being a part of that church. It was a church that welcomed them and allowed them to find a sense of home.

❖ **United Methodist Women**

Soon after my meeting with UMM, I was asked to come to a United Methodist Women's meeting. It was a lovely evening with a chance to visit with many of the ladies during the meal. Afterward I engaged them with a similar exercise to the one with UMM. I asked them what had attracted them to the church and what were the aspects of the church they still found meaningful? Like the men, they mentioned the importance of a caring fellowship.

❖ **Pastoral Reflection:** *Becoming Balcony People*

After conducting many small group discussions about the identity of the church, I decided to pose the same questions to the entire congregation. Some were now unsure of their church identity in the absence of their dynamic leader who had impacted the church's vision in so many ways. The reflection printed below was intended to help the congregation sort out that identity.

Becoming Balcony People

A few weeks ago five church leaders and I were asked to become "balcony people." Balcony people are ones who can view the church with fresh eyes, find purpose behind programs, vision beyond identity. Balcony people are those who can transcend the present reality and see ahead to what God is calling the Church to do – and in our case, who God is calling our particular church to become.

This first session had much to do with discerning who we are as a church in this present moment. Our group was asked to determine the distinctive qualities of our church. We, the leadership team, invite you to be a part of this process of discernment. Please jot down your answers and share them with the team.

- What first brought you to this church?
- What need(s) did it meet?
- What attribute, quality, or ministry do you hope the church never loses?
- What change would you most like to see in the church's future?

During the retreat one member of our group shared his image of our church. "It feels like home," he said. "It is a safe place, a place to belong, a place that brings a certain comfort despite everything else that happens, good or bad." I shared with him that I also sensed a deep level of intimacy and caring in this church, despite the fact that the church had grown into a fairly large church.

I am excited about our present time of discernment concerning our church, a time not only to think about what the church means to us individually, but also what it could mean to others if we were intentional about meeting their needs as well. Then perhaps we could work towards our church feeling like home to others and ensure that the level of intimacy and caring does not lessen with an influx of new members. And for those of us who venture to the balcony, we may discover even more – not only who we are, or even who we can become, but who God calls us to be.

I am very much a newcomer here at the church, but from what I have observed from "on high" (that would be from the balcony), and what I see brewing below, I am convinced that the best years of the church are not behind us, but in front of us. But before that happens, there is some work to do. We must first know who we are, who we desire to be, and who, with God's help, we can become!

In Faith, Justin

❖ Strategic Planning Seminar

One of the most providential experiences during my interim appointment was participation in a Strategic Planning Seminar that had previously been arranged by the former pastor. This seminar was attended by representatives from six healthy churches each bringing five lay persons along with their pastor. During the seminar there was time for the various churches to discuss issues among themselves. The time our group spent was extremely valuable.

The key issue of the first seminar concerned the identity of the church. Our group of six spent much of our time talking about our church's identity and we agreed with the conclusion of the UMM and UMW—that the church was primarily marked by being a caring community. Our group, however, added the aspect of zeal for mission—"*a caring community that welcomed and nurtured people coupled with a compassion that reached out to others.*"

What was perhaps more important was the discussion concerning the recent pastor's role in the formation of these distinctive qualities. She could not be credited with the most dominant aspect (a caring community) because that had been the dominant characteristic of the church before her arrival. What was obvious, however, was her zeal for mission that had been adopted by the church. The question at hand then became: "Was this zeal for mission now a characteristic of the church, or would this aspect of the church's life diminish or die without her presence?" We all agreed that concern for mission was now an indelible part of the church's identity.

A wonderful benefit to the seminar was my coming to know five of the church leaders and for us to share in significant discussion about the church, their beloved pastor, and our hopes for our church. That grounding and connection would prove to be valuable as I worked with these leaders in the future. I later used our consensus concerning our church's identity as a way to "mirror back to the congregation" what we believed to be their true identity.

❖ **Study Series: The Church's Identity Clarified**

Just as the Strategic Planning Seminar helped define our church's identity for the six who attended, the Study Series held in February would prove equally insightful to the church as a whole. This was due in part to the careful planning of the event. The associate and I met with the seminar leader who would also preach on two occasions. We talked about the subjects to be covered in the series and what we hoped would be accomplished. Fortunately, our objectives and his area of expertise were an exact fit. One key topic we wanted him to explore would be church identity.

In one of his messages, the leader made it clear to the congregation that he, and the conference as a whole, knew who they were. In developing his assertion, the preacher mentioned such things as "a caring congregation, a church committed to mission," but he added something extra to those already known characteristics—"a people of creativity and excellence." He made it clear that these characteristics were not those simply given or sustained by a pastor; they were now part of the church's DNA. In other words, these aspects of their identity do not change with a new pastor. He insisted that "what a pastor offers is not the DNA but his or her "fingerprints." The underlying message was: *"Your identity is clear and secure, even with the death of a beloved pastor and the arrival of new leadership."*

The preacher skillfully differentiated the deceased pastor's identity from the identity of the church while still acknowledging her significant influence. He then gave a touching tribute to her as he spoke of her life, character, courage, and the legacy she had left behind. Ten weeks after the beloved pastor's death, the preacher was able to revisit the issue of her loss and offer words of comfort. His poignant words about her, his gift of his honorarium in her memory combined to serve as a final loving tribute to her life and her ministry. For several members who seemed to be "stuck" in their grief process, this extended event brought a new level of healing.

Another key benefit of the speaker's time was his insights into how the church can maintain the strengths and valued aspects of its identity. How, for example, does a church continue to be welcoming and caring as it grows bigger? He gave concrete examples of how such behavior can become an intentional part of our individual and corporate church life. He was beginning to point the church beyond its identity toward its future vision—one that would include maintaining that sense of family and closeness even as it grew into a large church.

❖ Key Turning Point

I would cite the study series as a key turning point during my interim. It marked an official claiming of the church's identity while separating it from the powerful charisma of its former senior pastor, now deceased. It gave a final tribute to a most loving and gifted pastor. It served as a time of closure for many who had not yet been able to let go and move forward in their grief. It served as an initial warning that in order to maintain its unique character; the church would have to be intentional about having a sense of family as one of its goals. Just as important, the speaker with his emphasis on the uniqueness of each pastor's gifts and personality, helped prepare the congregation for new pastoral leadership.

STAFF ISSUES

❖ Staff Renewal

One of my early goals was to eventually lighten the mood of the staff meetings. I was convinced that it had been a long time since they had laughed and that such expression of our humanity was long over-due. On the occasion of our third staff meeting I told one of my favorite jokes which was sufficiently corny to inspire groans as well as smiles and sufficiently self-deprecating to allow laughter at me, if not the joke. My assessment: it worked!

I also continued to urge staff members to take time off and to continue to work on their grieving process. The staff was not yet through with their grieving, but their grief was no longer apparent to members of the congregation. The staff had not become a hindrance to closure for the congregation. Indeed, some like the associate continued to help people through sermon and individual conversation to move to that point where the memory of the former pastor brought to the surface at least as much joy as sadness. This balance of joy and sadness marks the beginning of grief running its course. The destination, however, is never fully reached.

At some point in my stay I felt the staff needed to be affirmed for all that they had done during the past two years. I wrote a tribute to them and read it to them during the staff meeting. The text of *Posting the Colors* follows.

First Interim

Posting the Colors

What can I say to you, the survivors of a long battle? Not enough, I'm sure. So many admired your captain, and rightfully so. She was magnificent even until the very end. She gave her all. I admire her and her witness, even though my time with her was brief. You have an infinitely greater loss, a void that can never be filled.

But today as I post the colors, I am not thinking about the one who made the ultimate sacrifice. Today I am thinking about those who have finished a long battle and have signed up for another tour of duty. I am thinking about those who for the past two years were in the trenches, going the second mile, covering the bases, working without the glory, working in loyalty to the captain and to the Cause—and who can question the greatness of our Cause?

I have been a captain myself, a wounded one who could not be a hundred percent. I know how much my troops covered for me. I know of their bravery, their quality work, their commitment to the Cause. And I also saw its toll on them. I knew of their battle-weary bodies and souls. I am grateful for them.

But today I am talking about you in case analogy is not your thing. You, the staff, are the focus of my tribute. I admire you for what you have done and are doing. I empathize with the weight you have carried and the delicate tightrope walks you have negotiated. I know it has been difficult, but I also hope you know it was worth it. The Cause was certainly worthy of your efforts. Your captain was worthy of your efforts. And your church deserved and needed no less than you were able to give. That, my friends, is no small consolation.

I do not presume that you did it perfectly. In the heat of battle we just do the best we can. But from the looks of the battlefield, and the health of the survivors, I must conclude that you did a very good job, a very good job, indeed.

So today I post the colors for you. They are not the traditional red, white, and blue. The colors I post are simple, symbolizing who you are, what you have done, and what I can expect of you. Today I post the colors for this staff: True Blue, True Blue. I salute you.

First Interim

❖ Securing Time Off

In March, the associate brought a concern to me about her work load. She had been given more and more responsibilities during the past two years. At this point she was the staff person for about seven major committees. We both agreed this was too much and a hindrance to her recovery from exhaustion and problematic to her present family life. After deciding together on a short-term solution, I sent a letter to the chairs of the seven committees asking them to excuse her from the next two monthly meetings while keeping her informed of future plans and decisions reached by the committees. The confidence in the plan rested in part on the strong leadership of each of the committees. The result of this decision was a sigh of relief from the associate, a word of thanks from her husband, and not one word of protest from committee chairs. Yes, the church can function without constant pastoral oversight.

❖ Staff Intervention

Another sticky issue arose concerning the staff. Without describing this issue in detail, one staff member had refused to be a team player and had exhibited from time to time hostile, rude or angry behavior that was unwarranted. After a major episode, I sat down with that staff person and made it clear that such behavior would have to stop. Further, I assured him that both staff parish and the new pastor would be thoroughly briefed of his behavior so they would not be blindsided nor be unacquainted with the history of various incidents of the past.

I strongly advised that he seek counseling since I believed his problems could not be eliminated solely by self discipline. I also shared with him my own personal struggles with anger and depression as a way of conveying both my empathy and my confidence in a positive outcome, given the proper approach.

Later I would have a follow-up meeting that would be less aggressive and more supportive. His behavior improved significantly but not without some lapses, one even on my last Sunday. I deferred that matter to the staff parish chair. I also thoroughly briefed the incoming pastor as to the nature of these issues.

An interim appointment provides an excellent opportunity to deal with difficult staff issues. It is far better that an interim pastor be able to make some tough calls and at times remove a troublesome staff member. If not, documentation can begin so that a new pastor will not have to start the process and possibly bear the brunt of backlash from church members.

CRUCIAL ISSUES

❖ The Congregation's Journey with Grief

When I first came to this interim appointment, I thought that the most important aspect of my ministry there, the one requiring the most time and emotional energy, would be to assist the congregation in the grieving process itself. The church, however, proved to be more resilient than I had thought, and with a few notable exceptions, dealt extremely well with their tragic loss.

One reason the congregation did as well as they did was that they were given theological insights into the tough questions that had been raised by their pastor's tragic illness and death. Another key was their ability to minister to each other. In general, the church did a remarkable job of facing their pastor's death and honoring her memory. They did so by living their own lives with courage and faith, an example she had certainly shared with the congregation in both word and personal example.

❖ Explaining the Appointive Process

One of my responsibilities as interim pastor was to make sure the congregation understood the appointive process within the denomination. The church's members were comprised of a large number of non-Methodist members, thus making further education quite necessary. Some members had even talked about sending in the name of the person they wanted as pastor. (We are not a called system and such a process is not appropriate.) I decided that I should write a letter sharing the process in hopes not only to correct misunderstandings but also to alleviate some of their concerns and fears.

❖ More than Grief: Emerging Issues

Halfway through my six-month interim appointment I began to realize that many other issues besides assisting a grieving congregation would require my attention and energy. Paramount among these issues were church finances and the need for growth in individual stewardship. Without improvement in this area the church's future would be in jeopardy. Other issues included claiming the church's identity, interpreting the former pastor's death and legacy, discovering a new vision for the church (something the Strategic Seminar would enable), reclaiming normalcy in church life, continuing to revitalize staff and lay leadership. Though assisting in the grief process was an immediate and critical concern, the success of the interim experience was even more tied to how well these other issues were addressed, so that the church would not simply be left in limbo until the new pastor arrived. Indeed, an interim pastor has, I believe, a greater ability to affect real change in the life of the church than a new minister whose every move will be evaluated at the onset.

STAGE THREE: MOVING INTO THE FUTURE

STEPS TOWARDS TRANSITION

In many ways, my job as interim pastor became much easier in the last two months. First, I had fewer tasks to accomplish. Second, much of the significant programming of the church would be lead by staff or key lay persons. One of my major responsibilities was to create a positive attitude in the church to receive the new pastor. After the new pastor was announced, I was able to say very positive things about him and his wife, since I had been his mentor pastor as he began ministry.

- ❖ **Meetings with the Appointed Pastor**

I called the new pastor and asked if it would be helpful to meet with him. We arranged to meet for lunch. In my meticulous way I had typed out two pages of notes of things I thought might be helpful to him. I refrained from sharing that, however, until he had had time to raise his concerns and ask his questions. I shared my goals for the rest of my time and offered **two key suggestions.**

- ❖ **Incoming Pastor Invited to Do Strategic Planning**

I suggested that he, rather than me, attend the next Strategic Planning Seminar which would take place prior to his coming to the church and while he continued to serve

Moving into the Future

his present appointment. I thought he should be there since the next session would deal again with church identity and then take a look toward the future. It would also give him an opportunity to meet five of our laity and give them a chance to come to know him. (He was able to attend, and did find the experience very helpful.) It was also helpful to the church since I would no longer be exerting my leadership but instead deferring such a role to the lay leadership and the future pastor.

❖ Interim Pastor Offers to do Stewardship Planning

The second suggestion was that I help create a stewardship program for the fall. If the church waited until he came in July it would already be behind schedule. Since finances were still in bad shape although they had shown great improvement, the stewardship program was of utmost importance. I shared with the incoming pastor the general ideas and organizational structure and he gave his blessing to proceed with the early planning.

After the new pastor arrived, there were minor changes to the program including a new theme, but the major parts of the plan stayed intact. I believe I helped save the new pastor time without dictating the final details of the program.

❖ Pictorial Directory

I also announced to the incoming pastor that one of my gifts to him would be a new pictorial directory that would assist him in learning the names of the congregation. It would be ready soon after his arrival in July. An additional benefit of the endeavor would be the correction of home and email addresses and phone numbers. The chairman of the directory committee and former membership secretary agreed to call all the inactives herself to check on their needs, correct information, and make them aware of the church's upcoming activities. During that process, she received promises of becoming active again from some and indications of membership changes from others. This process helped update all the membership information and designated over a hundred people who had joined other churches or wished to be withdrawn.

POSITIVE SIGNS OF VITALITY

During the last two months I began to see signs of new life. There was a good spirit in the congregation. The staff was energized and ready to pour themselves into their work. The church was certainly not in limbo. Signs of a new vitality were abundant.

❖ Easter Worship

The spirit of the four worship services on Easter Sunday was electric and positive. The services were well-received and the attendance surpassed that of the previous year by about 50 people. The service built on resurrection hope was a message needed for a church that had been devastated only months before. Easter was, indeed, a high moment for the life of the church!

❖ Reflections: Signs of Easter

To celebrate the impact of Easter upon the life of our church, I wrote a reflection that lifted the resurrection hope.

Signs of Easter!

Easter Sunday was such an exciting day as nearly 1700 people joined in the celebration of Christ's resurrection! The music was uplifting, the youth sunrise service creative and meaningful, and the overflow crowd of 814 at the 9:30 service a sight to behold. In all four services we joined our voices in celebration: "Christ is risen. Christ is risen indeed!"

What we Christians sometimes fail to remember is that every Sunday is a celebration of Easter. We worship on Sunday as our Sabbath in honor of the day of resurrection. We are not only Christians; we are Easter People, those who affirm not only life after death, but love over hate, hope over despair, victory over defeat. We believe that the resurrection means the gift of Christ's spirit to us, one that offers us comfort, guidance, and strength.

As Easter people I hope you can see the signs of new life all around you, especially in the life of this church. People are joining our fellowship. Members are giving generously to the budget, the building programs, and the many mission projects we undertake. We are moving into a new facility brought about by the extra-mile giving of our congregation. This new space offers a useful place for our creative school, our children's and music ministries as well as Sunday school space for adults. It is a wonderful building where children will learn, melodies will be sung, and Scripture will be interpreted and applied to daily life.

When I arrived in early December of last year, I did not expect to see such signs of growth and vitality by Easter morning. I suppose I underestimated both the strength of this congregation and the power of the Holy Spirit to bring healing and wholeness to so many who were grieving and weary. It is deeply rewarding to have witnessed this transformation. I am proud of you as a church and as a people of faith. I have great confidence in your commitment to serve God and to be a caring community of faith. I am honored to have served with you during this difficult and intimate time. I have been blessed by your graciousness and your willingness to move boldly into the future.

During the last few weeks with you (my last Sunday is May 31) I hope to share some of the basics of the faith – the role of giving, the experience and meaning of worship, the centrality of grace, the role of the clergy in the life of the church, and my choice of a Scripture text for the church to live by. I hope these sermons will offer a solid foundation for the transition to a new senior pastor family, one that I trust you will both warmly welcome and strongly support.

I am already anticipating my withdrawal pains as I leave this congregation. Seldom have I had the opportunity to minister with an entire congregation in such a loving and intimate way. You have allowed me once more to experience God's presence and power in the face of death through both the gift of God's Spirit and the compassion you have shown for one another and for me. I look forward to our remaining time together and trust that I will see even more signs of faith, hope, and love as, together, we seek to be Christ's Church.
Grace and Peace, Justin

❖ **New Member Sunday**

No one expected that after a mailing and a follow-up phone call that twenty-two adults and 20 children would completely fill the chancel area to join the church! Everyone who joined was aware that as interim pastor I would soon be leaving and that a new senior pastor would not be on board until the first of July. This means that these families were not joining because of a pastor but because of what they had experienced of the church itself. This record joining was a marvelous sign to the church membership that they were a community of faith that others wanted to join. What a Sunday!

❖ **Celebration of the New Building**

Only weeks later, the congregation processed to the new wing that had just been completed which would house the creative school, children and adult classes, and music ministries. During my brief interim, I had witnessed the completion of the sanctuary remodeling and the opening of this new wing. It was exciting to see this new beautiful and functional building from which new and old ministries would be launched.

❖ **Confirmation for the Youth**

On May 17 fifty-nine youth were confirmed and several of their parents were also brought into membership. This wonderful group of youth and their families was a testimony to a proven program of confirmation coupled with an outstanding youth program. It was inspiring to see signs that the future leadership of the church had already begun its training and recruitment.

STEWARDSHIP EMPHASIS

My emphasis on stewardship had many dimensions:
- First, I led by example offering to tithe my salary and to donate all profits from the sale of my book to the church budget.
- Second, I educated the finance committee about their responsibilities.
- Third, I preached on the meaning of giving making clear both the spiritual need to give as well as the realistic financial needs of the church.
- Fourth, I planned a complete stewardship program. I worked with the new stewardship chair, business manager, and associate in devising the next year's stewardship plan.
- Fifth, I sent out an extra-mile giving letter to help with the cash flow needs of the church. (It was a program that brought in over $30,000.)

(Text of the letter follows.)

Dear Church Member,

    This will be my last correspondence with you before my departure on May 31. Recently I have seen so many positive signs of the health and vitality of the church; great Easter attendance, a record number of new members on April 26 (20 adults and 22 children), 60 youth ready to join the church on Confirmation Sunday, the beautiful and functional new building, a positive mood in the life of the church, the best staff I have ever worked with, and a new senior minister coming in July with high energy and an outgoing spirit.

    Only one major hurdle remains for the church: to totally underwrite the cost of its ministry and mission. At the end of April, after staying barely in the black for several months, we have fallen behind about $10,000 with no cash reserves. Keep in mind that our present expenses are considerably less than when your new pastor comes in July and we resume full salary for the senior minister.

    In order to meet this present challenge, the church will need considerable extra-mile giving. The current level of giving cannot support our present level of expenses, even after every area of the church has kept spending low. (We have under-spent the budget by $20,000 so far this year.) Unfortunately, there are no reserve funds, no more places to cut.

    In view of our present situation, I trust that each family will prayerfully consider their giving to the church. I hope each family will also consider doing one of the following:

1. Pay all or part of your yearly pledge in advance to help with cash flow.

2. Give an extra gift equal to your monthly giving.
3. Make a substantial gift of $1,000, $5,000 or $10,000 to be placed in a reserve fund to be used when regular giving does not equal expenditures.
4. Make as generous an extra-mile gift as you can afford.

Recently, the church has received a substantial pledge paid in full for the year. Another member has pledged to give an extra $10,000 in June as part of a reserve fund. Such gifts are encouraging, but they will need to be matched with many, many others in order for the church to stay solvent and to continue its wonderful ministries that make such a difference in people's lives. If you are willing to make an extra-mile gift in the next two months, please earmark it *"extra-mile gift"* so that the finance committee can know of your commitment to the church's future.

I am very proud of the church and of its valuable ministry to the congregation, the surrounding community, and to needs around the world. I hope and pray that the members of the church will meet this present financial challenge and step boldly into the future.

In Faith, Justin

PHASING OUT MY LEADERSHIP

My goal in the last month of the church was to basically provide no significant leadership except through worship and preaching. My last exercise of leadership was to set up the stewardship program and that would not have my name on it as it went forward with implementation. During that last month, I did spend time trying to make sure I completed a last rotation of pastoral care needs. I gave the associate the last planning session of the staff and did not even attend the meeting. In general I began the task of turning over responsibilities to the staff and to the lay leadership. I was not a part of the Strategic Planning Seminar or of the follow-up meetings. My last month was a transition of becoming less visible and less influential in the life of the church. This would be one way to prepare the congregation for a new leader.

FINAL WORDS

❖ Last Sermons

My last major impact on the transition to the new leadership would be the last two sermons. The first, "How to Treat Your Minister," was designed to stress both the human nature of all clergy and at the same time the importance of the divine call. I encouraged the congregation not to expect a certain type of minister but to be open to the one God called and one duly appointed by the bishop. I urged the congregation to love and nurture the entire pastor family, offering both hospitality and friendship.

In my farewell sermon on Pentecost Sunday I offered Romans 12:9-18 as the text for the church to adopt as its text, reflecting both its identity and its calling. I expressed my gratitude for my time with them and my high expectations for their future. Like Paul, the time for my departure had come. It had been a great run. I was glad I had come. I would miss the wonderful people of this church.

❖ **Goodbye and Thank You (Final Letter)**

Moving into the Future

Dear Church Family,

As I leave after six months of being your Interim Senior Pastor, my heart is full and my life is enriched. I came to minister among you at a most difficult time, at the loss of a devoted and beloved pastor. From the outset, I was touched by the depth of your grief and despair. But I was also encouraged by the valiant spirit among staff and congregation alike. During these past few months I have observed a great transformation. You have emerged as a resilient church, still aware of your loss but now with a greater understanding of what faith, hope, and love can bring into being when shared amongst a caring congregation. Indeed, God has been with us in this journey of love and faith.

In the process of giving myself in ministry here, I have been amply rewarded by your appreciation and affirmation. I have never felt so affirmed in my ministry as in my time with you. You have affirmed my preaching, my pastoral care, my administration, even my character and witness. As I retire from full-time ministry once again, I take with me a sense of being well-received and loved. That is a send off worth all my time and energy.

Speaking of send-offs, Janette and I are so grateful for your many kind words, the flowers in our honor, the numerous gift cards, wonderful books, a gorgeous birdhouse to adorn our Colorado home, and an elegant reception in our new round room. Thank you for all the ways you have made us feel appreciated and loved. This church will always have a very special place in our hearts. As we go our separate ways, we leave parts of ourselves behind, and we take parts of you with us. Thanks for your many acts of kindness.

In gratitude,
Justin and Janette Tull

Second Interim

SECOND INTERIM

PHASE I: FROM HIGH ANXIETY TO IMPROVED MORALE

INITIAL ENCOUNTERS

❖ **Answering the Call** (First Meeting with Leadership)
After answering "yes" to the Bishop's request to serve, my district superintendent introduced me to a group of church leaders including the Staff Parish Relations Committee, some members of the Church Council, and various key leaders. I was most interested in their ideas of what had gone wrong to cause such a drop in giving and attendance (both down about a third) and in ascertaining what they wanted from me as the new interim pastor. It was obvious that they were in shock and very distraught. They seemed compelled to warn me about how bad things were and to determine if I thought things were hopeless. I

showed no sign of panic. I assured them I had been briefed on the full extent of their predicament.

I knew that the current turmoil was due in part to the actions and inactions of the former senior pastor (currently on leave). His level of effectiveness had been compromised by several significant factors—the illness and subsequent death of his mother, a painful change of appointment, and poor physical health. The congregation understood this but that did not prevent a high level of frustration. One person commented: "He never even met us." Another comment was equally telling. "When I came to worship I didn't feel it was my church." Changes had been made in worship that seemed disruptive or strange to many of the worshippers.

Near the end of the meeting I probed to see if anyone saw some positive elements to their current situation. One member quickly responded, "What you have in this room are the core people of the church. We are not going anywhere. You can count on us." Near the end of the meeting, I invited everyone there to be a part of a calming presence in the church. I expressed faith that their church was not a "sinking ship." We were going to make it. I closed the meeting with prayer lifting up both hope for the future and a call for us to "*be* the church."

❖ **Church Council Action**

In retrospect, the action of the Church Council before my official arrival was both wise and realistic. Since pledges had declined by about $250,000, they acted decisively and cut the budget by that amount, adopting a balanced budget. Key to their cost-cutting efforts was a renegotiation of the loan payment to their lending institution which agreed to an "interest only" payment for the next year.

- ❖ **Staff Parish Relations Committee (SPRC) Action**

Before taking office I met with the outgoing and incoming SPRC chairs. We agreed that even further budget cuts were in order. I concurred with the action of the committee to cut two staff members, a savings of $61,000. Without doing so, there was little hope of securing the associate position for the upcoming appointive process. Subsequently, the associate would be asked to have a key role in the youth program upon the departure of the youth director.

INITIAL OBSERVATION: TOTAL MELTDOWN

In my 38 years of ministry I had never observed such a drastic reduction of attendance and giving as the one taking place in my new appointment. In the past few months the church had experienced about a third reduction in giving and attendance. The morale of the church and staff was low. Almost every member I met those first few weeks was depressed about the church. Even many who were still attending the church admitted to me that they had strongly considered leaving. There were several issues involved and most laden with deep emotion. Some people were in grief over friends who had left the church. They wanted them to come back but were beginning to realize that most would not be returning. Some of the members were also sad that their church was in such a desperate condition and felt helpless to turn it around. A few felt guilty that they had not been able to minister to the senior pastor who was now on leave and would not be returning. Some feared that the removal of the senior pastor from the church would be seen as racially based, though they insisted that race was not a factor. Pervasive throughout the church was a very heavy anxiety for the church's future. Many feared the worse—that their church would simply not survive.

Early on, I had a suspicion that the "meltdown" was not simply caused by the actions or inactions of the newly appointed senior pastor but was due in part to other unresolved issues. Within a few weeks I had concluded that there were two other issues that heavily contributed to the present crisis and high anxiety level—confusion over the vision of the church and a "conflicted" worship identity. Add to all these factors the church's history of traumatic appointment changes and the current economic slump and you have the makings of a "perfect storm."

INITIAL STRATEGY

As I began my work I soon wrote down my initial strategy.

- *Reassure the congregation: "We are not a sinking ship!"*

From my initial meeting with leaders to my first week on the job I expressed confidence that the church was going to be all right. Yes, we were taking on water but we would not go under.

- *Exhibit a less-anxious presence*

In spite of being a *Type A* personality, I tried to remain calm, focused and confident. At the same time, I offered no false hope that we could regain what had been lost. It was a time to make adjustments and not to simply expect things to return to the way they were.

❖ *Work first with key leaders and staff*

I suggested to staff and key leaders that we would have to "heal" before the church could follow suit. We needed to be a less-anxious presence committed to work toward recovery. We would need to be the first ones to exhibit hope.

❖ *Get to know the congregation*

Though leadership would be a key to recovery, I needed to bring a calming presence to the congregation at large. I committed myself to learning names, visiting with the congregation before and after church, and visiting the sick and shut in.

❖ *Use preaching as a way to address the present situation*

Preaching would be a primary way I could address some of the issues facing the church. I would also have to balance addressing the needs of the church with addressing the individual needs of members of the congregation. Indeed, the individual health of the church was linked to the spiritual health of the members.

❖ *Introduce weekly reflections to reach entire congregation*

In an effort to reach not only active members but also those who had recently left the church, I initiated a weekly column in the church email. I used this forum to address all the major issues facing the church.

DIAGNOSTIC GOALS

In order to be an effective interim pastor, I would need to address the issues listed. Eventually the church would have to come to its own conclusions.

o Discern the various causes for the meltdown

- Discern the key identity of the church
- Discern the vision of the church
- Discern the worship identity of the church

In an effort to gain insights into these important issues, I met in small groups with leaders, staff, and church members. I asked them directly what factors they thought contributed to the melt down. I also asked what had attracted them to the church and had compelled them to stay when so many had left. This latter question spoke directly to the issue of church identity. Their answers, whether from new members or charter members, were markedly the same. They had joined the church because of its caring quality, its sense of family. Their answers to the vision question, however, had little consensus and, at times, were even contradictory. Charter members spoke of a "regional church" and a target group of seekers. Newer members had no notion of the regional church idea and were, in fact, attracted to the church in great part because of its smaller size and sense of family. They had no vision of the church becoming much larger, nor would they welcome such a change.

The search for a worship identity was even more problematic. This was due in part to the wide variety of worship styles practiced by the congregation in its three distinctive church services. The associate pastor, music director, and I did our best to assess the worship needs and tastes of the congregation. During those first weeks of planning worship together, we strove to offer some sense of continuity to the worship tradition. Our problem was, as newcomers, we were not sure what that tradition was or whether newer members had embraced one particular tradition. Early on, I decided that a worship survey was the only objective way to determine the current worship tastes of the congregation. I decided it needed to be taken in three separate groups, one for each of the three Sunday morning services.

DIAGNOSING THE MELTDOWN

After visiting with countless church members and spending much time in reflection, I still cannot explain all of the causes of the church's "meltdown." What I can say with certainty is that the cause cannot be placed solely on any one factor or any one person. That having been said, two key areas of dissatisfaction can be traced to the previous senior pastor, who, in his defense, was in the midst of many personal crises at the time of his appointment.

The first issue was the pastor's failure to involve himself with his new congregation. Having stated publically that he was unhappy with being moved from his previous appointment, his behavior soon mirrored that message by failing to visit with church members either before or after worship. Soon he would be absent from the congregation because of the illness and later the death of his mother. Subsequently his own declining personal health left him unable to continue in ministry, resulting finally in being put on leave. This left a void of leadership at the top. Despite valiant efforts on the part of the associate and other members of the staff, church members felt adrift with no one in authority to take the helm.

A second factor may have been even more devastating. The senior pastor brought with him a new style of worship—one that did not match any of the three styles

Second Interim

of worship services already in place. In every church, even minor changes in worship can cause major problems, at least for some. In this church, where worship styles had long been a point of contention, these recent changes, coupled with other frustrations, would become a major stumbling block. Some claimed that when they went to worship it did not feel like their church. The sense of familiarity was gone.

These two issues seemed to be the crux of the membership's dissatisfaction with the senior pastor—lack of leadership and involvement coupled with the disruption of worship tradition. Even so, the extent of the fallout cannot be totally understood without looking at some long-standing issues. Each one of these other factors, I believe, played a significant role in the extent of the melt down that occurred. In fact, these other factors may have already contributed to the church showing some signs of decline or stagnation even before the new senior pastor began his appointment.

❖ Appointive Process Issues

In my experience in ministry I have never known of a church where every appointment change had resulted in conflict within the church. Though there had been only three senior pastor changes, each had been fraught with tension and conflict. This cannot be explained simply by the high number of members from non-Methodist backgrounds, those unfamiliar with our itinerate system. What was a key factor, I believe, was the sense on the part of the congregation that they had no control in the appointive process. The last appointive process (prior to the meltdown) seemed to illustrate the church's frustration. The decision was made to move both the senior pastor and the associate at the same time, eliminating any clergy continuity. That lack of continuity would be especially problematic since the new senior pastor, for a variety of factors, was unable to relate well to the congregation. The new associate, though willing and able to do so, was starting from scratch. In worship there was also no sense of continuity. The music director had some knowledge of the worship tradition, but that understanding was limited since he had been on staff only a short time. It is not surprising that worship, which subsequently underwent several significant changes, became a source of frustration for several of the members.

❖ **Vision Confusion**

As surprising as it may seem, I suspect that "vision confusion" was at the heart of much of the underlying tension in the church and a significant factor in pastor approval or disapproval. There was once a clear vision of what distinguished this church from other churches. In its early years it was not markedly Methodist. "Seekers" were its major target group. It was innovative in worship, built on the talents of its founding pastor. And its vision was to be a "regional church" and based on the large church plot, one of comparable size. After each change in pastoral leadership that vision did not seem to be redefined or reclaimed by the church or the new members who had more recently joined. The church eventually became more markedly United Methodist, the worship became less unique and a bit more traditional, its vision less apparent, and the "unchurched" were no longer the key target group. The surrounding culture had also changed with many large non-denominational churches targeting the "unchurched," and doing so with some degree of success. Soon this church, once poised to become a church with regional appeal, looked more and more like a typical neighborhood church.

This "vision confusion" would also lead to "worship confusion." The church would no longer be the worship innovator, so what was its form of worship? Was it still trying to be the innovative worship experience that it had with its founding pastor? What about the many who had joined the church in the last five years? Had they been attracted by the music and style of worship or something entirely different? What was the identity of the church, what was its worship tradition, and what was its vision?

- ❖ **Identity Versus Vision**

My conviction was that the church's identity had changed significantly from its early beginnings. True, certain aspects of the church's identity had remained constant. Soon after my arrival I concluded that the church was "a diverse and caring community marked by a zeal for mission." That part of its identity had been present from the beginning. But the church was no longer markedly different from other churches, either United Methodist or non-Methodist. The present church no longer primarily targeted seekers or the unchurched as had first been the case. It could no longer boast of a unique worship experience. It was no longer fast growing or on tract to be a "regional church." (I am told that it was once one of the fastest-growing churches in the area.) Now, in the midst of the present church crisis, the goal was not to become a large church; the goal was simply to survive.

My impression was that the average church member and certainly those who had joined recently had no notion of a vision of becoming a regional church. To find people who spoke of a large regional church, one would have to talk to long-time members. In fact, what had attracted most members to the church in recent years was precisely its "non-regional" nature. That is, many who joined did so in lieu of joining the many regional church options in the area. They liked the church's smaller size and its sense of family. If the church were to ever become a regional church, it would have to change its present identity or find ways of maintaining its sense of closeness despite becoming larger.

❖ **Failure to Grow**

In the minds of some of the members—primarily long-time members—failure to grow was seen as a failure to fulfill the church's vision and mission. To be located on a large plot of land while having a modest church plant and high indebtedness seemed to signal a failed dream. The "meltdown" was perhaps more devastating to some because it seemed an end to that vision or dream. But perhaps it could become a blessing in disguise if it forced the church to shape a new vision of who they are called to be.

❖ **Disenfranchisement**

When I arrived at the church, the feeling that seemed to permeate the entire congregation was a sense of disenfranchisement. It certainly applied to the appointive process where many felt they had no input and no control. It also applied to worship since a senior pastor had the power to change everything without regard to church tradition or the worship preferences of the congregation. The feeling of disenfranchisement even applied to the youth program where parents had little say as to what was offered for their youth. Parents of the youth had experienced constant changes of youth directors with little or no continuity in the program. I suspect that many who left the church in the past several years, and even some just prior to my coming may have done so because the youth program failed to meet their needs. This was a church that felt it had little control over its future. Other people were making decisions either without their input or with seeming little regard for it.

ADDRESSING THE ISSUES

❖ **Preaching Plan**

Perhaps the most important means of affecting change in the congregation's life is the sermon. The first few sermons would address key issues that the congregation was presently facing. Like the apostle Paul, I tried to apply the gospel to the current situation at hand—to offer some pastoral advice. My first message was the one I thought they most needed to hear.

➢ *Forgetting What Lies Behind!*   Philippians 3:12-14

Paul's message was a wonderful way to begin the New Year as individual Christians. But his message was also great advice to a church overly concerned with its past and unable to move into the future. This church desperately needed to forget the past (it could never return to where it was) and to look to the future with fresh eyes.

❖ **First Letter to the Congregation**

This letter was to introduce myself to the congregation and assure them of my commitment to be their pastor. I admitted the seriousness of the challenge ahead and invited them to join me in a "journey of healing, reconciliation, and renewed hope." The text of the letter follows.

Second Interim

Dear Church Family,

As most of you know by now, I have been assigned as your Interim Senior Pastor. I will begin my time with you this coming Sunday. In the months ahead, I will be in the office all day Mondays and Tuesdays and Wednesdays until noon (except when on pastoral calls). In addition I will attend many of the key evening meetings. Thursdays and Fridays will be reserved for sermon preparation and time away.

It is important that everyone understand that "interim" does not mean a time of "limbo." We will not be marking time until the new senior pastor arrives in July. Instead, we will be intentionally engaged in some hard work of transition. We, no doubt, differ as to exactly what has happened to our church over the past several months and what is our identity as a church. But regardless of how we analyze our past or describe our identity, our future action needs to be united as a community of faith. This is not a time for blaming but a time to move toward reconciliation and understanding by listening and caring – in short, by being the kind of faith community we have always desired for our church family. After meeting with the church leadership, I am convinced that this year holds much promise for this unique congregation.

And though I am called an "interim" and my time with you limited, I plan to do my best to get to know you on a personal level, to listen to your concerns, and to be available for pastoral care. I also pledge my leadership for the church and staff during the next several months. I commit to sharing in sermon what I believe to be the word of God for this day and this time. My first two sermons will come from Paul's letter to the church at Philippi, a place my wife I were privileged to visit last year. I invite you to use this short letter of Paul's as your devotional reading as you begin the new year.

As your new leader I do not claim to have all the answers, nor can my efforts—however intentional and sincere—bear much fruit without your full support and involvement. I believe I have been called to be your pastor. I hope and pray that most of you feel called to be the church, here and now in this place, in the midst of problems and disappointments. The call to be the church is not unlike the commitment of marriage which asks one to continue to love and cherish each other in better or worse circumstances, in richer or poorer times. The work of the church and the specific calling of this church deserve no less from us.

Please join me in a journey of healing, reconciliation and renewed hope as together we step into the new year as the people of God. May God guide and direct us on our journey.

In Faith, Justin

Second Interim

❖ Pastoral Reflections

This early reflection piece was my first pep talk to the congregation. Without denying the problems or offering false expectations, I shared the positive signs I saw within the life of the congregation. (The text of the reflection follows.)

Gtah @Our Church

When I was a student in Hendrix College, the president had a saying he repeated often, so often, in fact, that it was changed into an acronym – GTAHAH (Ga tah' ha –Good things are happening at Hendrix!) After having served here for two weeks, I find myself having a similar mantra about our church. After working with the staff and key leaders, meeting many of you, and getting a feel for the identity of this church, I must say quite honestly, "Good things are happening at our church."

To make such a statement does not mean I am unaware of problems, frustrations, and disappointments that have affected almost everyone in the church. Simply put, as an outsider becoming an insider, I can see signs of hope and progress that some of you may be unable to see. Permit me to share a few.

One of the first things that impressed me about the church was the diversity of membership—a diversity that has been intentional rather than a product of demographics or transition. Such diversity of age, race, and background is far too rare in churches across America. I celebrate such openness to one another, acknowledging at the same time that we have not yet arrived as a completely loving and welcoming congregation.

It also took me only a week to discover that this church is a "hands on" church. I observed some twenty people having fun, saving money, and putting in sweat equity by removing all the old carpet before the new carpet was installed. As the church becomes larger, hopefully that "hands on" quality will continue to be evident through involvement in mission, service,

Second Interim

and all forms of church life. Such a "hands on" spirit is really not about what we do physically but rather relates to the level of our involvement.

Perhaps most encouraging of all, I have discovered a core group of leaders and followers who are totally committed to the life and mission of the church. For those of you who have worried about the church's future in the midst of declining attendance and significant reduction in giving, I assure you that the core is ready and able to begin the journey to stability and new growth. Two families, just this week, have expressed their readiness to become a part of this congregation.

To their credit, the Finance committee, Staff Parish Relations Committee, and the Church Council have been realistic about the present financial base of this church. After a significant drop in pledges, the budget has been slashed and some staff positions eliminated. I fully expect such low giving trends to be reversed in the months ahead. But until then, our present budget goals are realistic and attainable. To do my part, I am serving at half salary and will be tithing my income. I encourage all members to give sacrificially at this time of transition.

So, I am back to my original thought – "Good things are happening at our church." Maybe we should change our email address to GTAH@OURCHURCH.

Grace and Peace, Justin.

❖ **Reflections (continued)**

I continued to use pastoral reflections to emphasize key matters of the church. (A summary of two of these reflections follows.)

➢ *Mission Matters!*

By this time I had already discerned that the church had a strong mission identity. I used that strength as an incentive to come to worship that coming Sunday when a pastor of a local outreach ministry was to preach. My purpose was to get the church to claim its mission identity and make it even stronger. After all, *mission matters!*

➢ *We Are a Family Together!*

This unashamedly promotional reflection was aimed at getting as many as possible to attend a joint service, followed by a church-wide dinner. This would be a rare opportunity for the three separate worship congregations to be together. It would be a time to gain some new energy and a positive spirit. The morning turned out to be a high moment in my first month and, I believe, a turning point in the life of the church.

STATE OF THE CHURCH

After one month as interim senior pastor, I was very pleased with the progress that had been made. A few families that had stopped coming returned. Morale had drastically improved and the joint worship service and fellowship meal at the end of January had high energy and great interaction among the members. There was still some anxiety about the future and some sadness over the loss of active membership, but there was no longer panic or

Second Interim

despair. People finally understood that the ship was not sinking, and no longer taking on more water!

Though progress had been made, there were still plenty of challenges ahead. Giving level, even with the drastically reduced budget, was still not enough, though close. Attendance had improved but was still significantly behind previous years' figures.

PHASE II: *STABILIZATION AND RENEWED HOPE*

MEANINGFUL WORSHIP: A KEY TO RECOVERY

As with most churches, worship stands as the most important aspect of church life. For this particular interim appointment the worship experience was even more essential and problematic.

❖ **Early Worship Changes**

Even though changing the worship service is always fraught with danger, I felt that we should make some changes to bring back a sense of familiarity. This meant in part to discontinue some of the recent changes made by the previous pastor and to return to the worship tradition known by most of the congregation. We did risk making our own minor changes in order to improve flow, unity of theme, and create a more familiar feel to the service. We used repetition of elements and more familiar music to also raise the comfort level in a church where worship had become a volatile issue. I added a call to worship and silent prayer as traditional touches to both the traditional service and the blended service. These changes seemed to be well-received, especially the addition of silent prayer which added a meditative aspect to the service. I also dropped the newly added stewardship scripture and music between the scripture and the sermon as both did not seem to add much to the service and interrupted the flow and worship theme.

Most importantly, the worship planning team of interim senior pastor, associate pastor, and music director were committed to a unity of theme and smooth transitions in the service. We also learned to listen carefully to each other in order to find a consensus in worship elements that we thought would be effective. Even so, none of us had been there long enough to really know what were the most meaningful aspects of worship for this congregation.

- ❖ **Worship Survey**

Apart from my contribution as preacher, perhaps my most important gift to this congregation was my decision to do a worship survey. This survey would help determine the worship preferences of the congregation. I decided to do the survey using each worshipping community as a group. This would give a consensus by worship service groups as to what was meaningful to them. The elements of the service would be numerically ranked clearly differentiating the most meaningful down to the least meaningful elements.

This instrument would be used in several ways. First, it would be used to inform the church as to its worship identity or more accurately, its various worship identities. Second, I promised that it would be a base line for clergy to use in planning worship. I did not suggest that congregational preference would dictate exactly how worship was done but rather that the pastor would now know in advance aspects of worship that were the most meaningful for each worshipping community. Third, since the survey followed the three different worshipping services (blended, contemporary, and traditional), the results would be helpful in making decisions as to how to reduce the number of services and establish a new schedule.

❖ **Decision Making Process for Cutting a Service**

Having already experienced drastic reduced attendance in all three services and facing additional reduction from summer absences, it was apparent to me and the staff that reducing the number of services might be a way to increase the numbers in the remaining two and boost the energy level of worship. I first floated the idea to the Church Council and they agreed with the need to cut back a service. In the questionnaire responses a large majority favored going to two services. The problem arose when people realized it might be *their* service that was cut. We set out a process for making the decision as to which worship services would continue and what the new schedule would be.

First, using the worship survey data, members of the worship committee task force would make a recommendation as to which service should be terminated. Second, a subcommittee of the Education Committee would look at the issue of scheduling and determine what would be the best schedule to promote small groups and the growth of the Sunday School program. Third, these two

Second Interim

groups would combine with representatives from the church and Church Council to form one larger task group that would make a final recommendation to the Church Council. The Church Council would in turn make a recommendation to the church for a vote on April 11.

In the process of making the decision, there were those who attended the contemporary service (the one eventually recommended to be cut) who expressed displeasure with the decision. After expressing disappointment, many from the contemporary service were later convinced that eliminating the contemporary service would make possible a renewal of the Sunday School. (The contemporary service and Sunday School both met at 9:45.) An important part of the rationale for the elimination of the contemporary service was the fact that the blended service contained almost all of their favorite aspects of worship. The assumption was that those who liked the contemporary worship service could find in the blended service a new worship home.

❖ Key Reflection on Worship Identity

I used the church newsletter to share my understanding of worship and my perceptions concerning the church's worshipping traditions. (Reflection on worship follows.)

Discerning Our Worship Identity

In its early years, this church had a unique style of worship, dependent for the most part on the special gifts of the founding pastor. I am sure that many people were attracted to the church because of its unique and dynamic worship. Since that time, the worship and music styles of the church have taken many different forms in order to reach people with different worship preferences and to reflect the various worship styles of each subsequent senior pastor.

During my first few weeks at the church, I became aware of a high level of anxiety concerning worship and music styles. Various changes in worship and music through the years had resulted in frustration for some and a loss of normalcy for others. For some, the feeling at home in the worship service was lost. But what remains unclear to me is the actual worship identity of the congregation. What is our worship home? For the past several years the solution to the diversity of worship tastes has been to offer three different worship services in hopes of meeting different worship preferences: traditional, contemporary, and blended (a combination of the first two). Though this does help meet different worship needs, it has not helped clarify who we are as a worshipping community. For example, do the people worshipping at the early service like its traditional form or do they just like the early worshipping time?

As one who has the primary responsibility for planning and conducting worship, I want to have a clearer understanding of the worship preferences of this congregation not only for our

Second Interim

present benefit but as a baseline for future decisions in worship.

I hope the survey results will be an important tool for us and for the new senior pastor coming in July. I believe that though clergy are in charge of worship by virtue of their ordination and position, that they should always be sensitive to the unique worship practices and styles of any given congregation. Clergy should not simply insist that worship be done only *our way*. On the other hand, clergy must ensure that worship practices are appropriate, theologically sound, and reflect some of our own unique gifts and graces.

In order to plan meaningful worship, the clergy and worship committee would like to know more definitively the worship tastes, preferences, and needs of our congregation. To that end, a questionnaire has been designed to allow you to express your worship preferences. Please understand that this will be a valuable feedback tool, but not a rigid mandate. For example, if you as a church vote to cut the sermon from the worship service, that will probably not happen.

This Sunday at all three services you will have an opportunity to fill out a worship preference questionnaire. This same instrument is already available on our website. The deadline for completion of the survey is Sunday, March 14. Since all results will be tabulated through the website version, it is our hope that most people will complete the form in that way. Otherwise someone will have to manually enter it for you using the on-line form. And, yes, only one entry per person.

Guided by the questionnaire results, an important vote will take place on Sunday, April 11, following the 11:00 service.

Stabilization and Renewed Hope

At that time the Church Council will present a proposal or proposals for a new worship and Sunday School schedule that best meets the present needs of this congregation. Hopefully, this decision will provide some stability and continuity to the worship experience at the church, not only now, but for several years to come.

My hope and prayer is that after sharing our individual preferences for worship we can then be about the business of worshipping as the body of Christ, less concerned now about the *way* we worship and more concerned *that* we worship, and worship together. Indeed, we may even find a new unity in our diversity!

Grace and Peace, Justin

Second Interim

❖ Lenten Plan

The Lenten season provided a great opportunity for the church to grow spiritually and find a sense of comfort and fulfillment to replace the recent feelings of frustration and anxiety. To supplement a series of well-planned worship services during the Lenten season, the education committee introduced a series of Lenten studies. These would not only foster spiritual growth, but also provide meaningful interaction between the members. I offered a study based on my book, *Why, God Why?* which attracted some 25 participants. The over-all response to the studies was a very positive one and proved to be a turning point in church life and morale.

The special services that were planned, e.g. Ash Wednesday, Palm Passion Sunday, and Maundy Thursday were especially well-received. The Maundy Thursday service was particularly successful in engaging church members to be a part of a dramatic presentation of the Last Supper. The music director could also claim a victory in utilizing local high school students to provide outstanding orchestral music for the service, all without budgetary expense. In a church where one worship style rarely garnered broad-based support from the entire congregation, these worship services united us into one worshipping body. Worship style did not seem to be an issue, since these services represented a marked change in the norm (usually a cause of contention) and were decidedly more liturgical (not the flavor of choice of the congregation). Perhaps when worship is meaningful and draws us into a spirit of closeness to God and an awareness of God's truth, the style of worship is not the most important thing.

Easter Sunday proved to be a dramatic climax to the Lenten season, as well it should be. Church attendance for the first time in months came very close to the numbers of previous years. There was great excitement as we celebrated the resurrection of Jesus Christ. The church was, indeed, experiencing a bit of a resurrection of its own.

❖ **Preaching Plan**

The preaching plan for Lent took on a new focus. The emphasis would not be on the church and its problems, but rather on the individual life of a Christian. Lent, in fact, lends itself to an emphasis on the Christian life and behavior. As interim pastor, I wanted to share with the congregation some of the essential teachings of the faith. Where better to turn than the Sermon on the Mount, the largest collection of Jesus' teaching in the New Testament?

REFLECTIONS

During the Lenten season, I focused three of my reflections on the subject of worship.

➢ *Prepare to Worship*

In the face of worship squabbling and prevalent worship consumerism, I reminded the congregation that ultimately worship is our individual responsibility. What we bring to worship is equally important to what the worship leaders bring to us. Ultimately, the congregation is not to be the audience of worship. God is.

Second Interim

> *Discerning Our Worship Identity* (Text shared earlier.)

In this article I traced part of the church's worship history and invited the congregation to be a part of determining our worship identity. I offered the worship survey as a means of establishing a base line for our worship experience.

> *Our Worship: Unity and Diversity!*

This article focused on some of the findings of the worship survey. In all three services, attendees expressed highest marks for Holy Communion, concerns shared by the pastor, and greeting one another in Christian love. Though other responses suggested great diversity, these important elements of worship reflected quite accurately the central identity of the church—that we find unity within our diversity by being an open and caring community of faith. Meaningful worship in this church should not forget our unity nor ignore the richness of our diversity.

GETTING OUR HOUSE IN ORDER

❖ **New Member Sunday**

It is not surprising that in the midst of our inner turmoil, no one had joined the church. I decided after several months it was time to see if there were those who were ready to join. Letters were sent out; phone calls and announcements made. In the weeks that followed several new members were added to our community of faith. It was a sign of hope that people were joining our fellowship without knowing who would be the new senior pastor.

Stabilization and Renewed Hope

❖ **Supporting Mission Identity**

Having realized early that the church had a strong emphasis on mission, I wanted to do everything I could to support that important emphasis of church life. I brought my Haiti health kits, wore Haiti wrist bands, and celebrated the signs of mission support by the congregation. My best "hands on" contribution was working two weekends for Amigos Days—an outreach program of the United Methodist Church. It was fitting that on my last Sunday at the church I was honored with the gifts of an Amigos shirt and a Habitat for Humanity shirt, both mission ministries close to my heart.

❖ **Transformation Decision**

The church had been a part of a program called Transformation for churches being renewed and strengthened. Given the church's present state, I wondered if they should continue in the program and, if so, under what timetable. After meeting with the Conference liaison for the program, the associate and I both agreed that the program would be a good thing for the church to continue. In recommending the program to the Church Council I provided them with the following reasons we should consider continuing to participate:

- It would give the laity and staff a voice and involvement with the visioning of the church.
- The process would not intensify until September when major data gathering would occur.
- The plan would not place the responsibility of setting a vision on the new senior pastor but would

be properly shared with the congregation, thus creating ownership.
- o Staying in the program would help facilitate shedding the "vision confusion" that presently serves as a detriment to the church's future.

STEWARDSHIP WORK

Because of the drastic and appropriate action of the Church Council in cutting the budget by $250,000, I did not have to make a plea for money to the congregation during the first few months. The realistic action of the Council gave the church time to heal and to regain a positive spirit. No one wants to give to a sinking ship. My first stewardship efforts were to educate the Finance Committee of their role and to ensure that the church staff was frugal in spending during the tight budget times. Listed below are specific things I did during my tenure to bolster giving and stewardship.

❖ **Personal Example**

Several years ago in a stewardship seminar I was told that the personal example of the pastor was often instrumental in increasing giving. Since then I have publically shared my own stewardship story, not as a means of glorifying myself but as a simple witness to the value of giving as a spiritual discipline. After arriving at the appointment, I soon made it public that I was tithing my salary. I also pledged to donate $3.00 to the budget for each of my books sold. This took away the notion that I was hawking my books to make a profit and suggested that I was concerned about supporting the budget. At the end of my tenure I gave my last two week's salary to plant rows of roses in front of the large church sign. Now passersby cannot miss noticing the church. This was my goodbye thank you.

❖ Educating the Finance Committee

At the first Finance Committee meeting I explained that the purpose of the Finance Committee, despite rumors to the contrary, was not to simply control the purse strings of the church. True, there were times when they might have to recommend cutbacks or suggest caution in spending. (They had done this in a responsible way during the start of the crisis.) Their first goal, however, was to ensure that giving matched the budget needs instead of making a budget to match giving. Part of their role was to help promote stewardship and to increase giving.

Second, I assured them that with the reduced budget we should be able to meet that budget commitment. I shared my general philosophy of church finance: to keep the congregation informed at all times of the needs of the church. If the budget was realistic, and if the church was healthy, the money would come in. Though the church was not healthy at the time, I believed it could soon be on the road to recovery. We needed to give the church a chance to turn things around in the next two months. If more drastic means were needed to secure the necessary funding, we could inaugurate programs at that time.

❖ Letters to New Members about Giving

When each new member joined the church, I sent a letter urging them to become active in the life of the church and encouraging them to make a pledge and to consider the disciplined giving of a tithe. Several of the new members did

Second Interim

respond by returning the pledge card and supporting the church.

- ❖ **Introduce Extra-Mile giving Program**

After two months, the giving level was not quite reaching the drastically reduced budget. I sent out a letter urging the members to do one or more of three options: to give extra, to become current in their giving, or to make a pledge if they had not already done so. I asked that they designate any extra-mile giving so that the Finance Committee would know that these funds were beyond pledged giving. During the next month, the program netted $8,700 extra giving and also resulted in increased pledges. (The text of the letter follows.)

Dear Church Member,

I hope you have seen signs that our church is once again a vibrant church. Even through our recent crisis, we never lost our deep caring for one another. That trait sets us apart from so many churches. Few can match the sense of family and unifying compassion that we enjoy here.

What has been missing until recently is a positive attitude for our future. A drop in both attendance and giving levels initially led to doubts about our future and a high level of anxiety. For most of us, that uneasy feeling is now gone. New members, great attendance at Easter (543), and the constant influx of visitors all suggest great promise. Our new senior pastor is excited about coming here and when she arrives in July will be ready with high energy, fresh ideas, and a vision of the future. When she joins our gifted and dedicated staff, there should be new enthusiasm and a positive spirit among the members.

But before that time comes, our church needs to get its house in order and to once again underwrite its current ministries and expenses. At present, we are not meeting our drastically cut 2010 budget—but we are close. Our cash flow is precariously low and we are paying bills on a week to week basis.

In order to meet this present challenge, we will need to increase our general giving level. Though some are out of work and unable to contribute significantly, others have the capability of giving extra, especially at this crucial time. It is hoped that we will not only be able to meet the present budget but in the near future begin to grow our finances so that all or part of the staff

Second Interim

positions that were cut in 2010 can eventually be reinstated. Our present staff and lay volunteers are to be commended for holding down the fort in the meantime, especially in the areas of youth and children's ministries.

In an effort to address this present shortfall, the Finance Committee is asking that every member consider making a special *extra-mile gift* during the next few months. There are, in fact, several different ways you can help undergird our important ministries:

- Give a gift equal to your normal monthly giving.
- Make a substantial gift of $1,000, $5,000, or $10,000.
- Make as generous an extra-mile gift as you can presently afford.
- Stay current with your giving.
- Make a pledge for this year if you have not done so.

Now is the time to evaluate what our church means to us. It is time to invest significantly in all the current programs and ministries that make such a difference in your lives and the lives of our community. If you are willing to make an *extra-mile gift* during the next two months, *please earmark your check, "Extra-mile Gift"* so that the Finance Committee can monitor anticipated giving and maintain the church budget. We hope you will join with us as we invest in our church's future.

In Faith,
Interim Senior Pastor   Finance Chair   Church Council Chair

STATE OF THE CHURCH: CAUTIOUS OPTIMISM

Easter Sunday was a sure sign that the church had turned the corner. Attendance was almost up to old levels even without many of the members who had left the church. Giving was also at an all-time high since my arrival. In general, by Easter all the indicators were up, plus there was a perceivable change in morale. Now the church had a cautious optimism. We were out of rehab and gaining strength. Or to put it another way: "We were not sinking, had made necessary repairs, had all hands on deck and were moving forward. We just needed a few more coordinates in order to determine our future destination."

Two challenges lay before us: to be able to drop a worship service without major fallout and to properly prepare for the arrival of a new senior pastor. The church was in hopes of having the first smooth transition for a change of pastors in its history! (That positive transition later happened!)

Second Interim

PHASE III: *PREPARING FOR THE FUTURE*

FINAL STEPS

❖ Staff Renewal

In my first staff meeting I had urged all staff members to make plans to take some much-needed time off. By this time several had taken time away and the rest had made plans to do the same. In addition, I urged the associate to take time off to plan sermons for the month of June when she would be solely in charge. (I would leave the end of May and the new senior pastor would not arrive until July.) The associate took some time off and came back with sermon plans and more energy than I had seen since my arrival. I was also able to lighten my own work load during my last month.

❖ Final Worship Decision

After the eleven o'clock service on April 11, about 120 people stayed to hear the proposal for the change of schedule which included dropping the 9:45 contemporary service. One of the major arguments was that this new schedule would allow a greater emphasis on the Sunday School program which was crucial if the church was to foster small groups and enhance the sense of community that was a key part of its Church identity. After discussion and one or two negative comments, a vote was taken. Only three people voted against the proposal though there might have been a few who abstained. In the weeks that followed only one family may have discontinued coming to worship as a result of the change. In the weeks that followed, overall attendance remained somewhat the same with increases in the two remaining services offsetting the cancellation of the 9:45 service. Until my departure some six weeks later I never heard any negative comments about the major change in our worship services and the new schedule. I attribute the success and lack of conflict to a long and open process coupled with the objective data of the worship survey. Had the worship decision been made by clergy or staff without input from the congregation, I am convinced that the church would have had another meltdown. It would have also been one more experience of disenfranchisement.

❖ **Sunday School and Small Groups**

Having successfully made a decision to cancel the contemporary service without a major reaction from the congregation, I wanted one more victory. I wanted to have a measureable gain in the Sunday School program to *justify* the change of schedule. During the next few weeks letters were sent out to those who had attended the 9:45 service urging them to pick another service and inviting them to be a part of the Sunday School program. I wrote reflections on the importance of small groups and called members of my Lenten study group inviting them to be a part of Sunday School which now had two new classes. On May 16, during the Sunday School hour, each of the Sunday School class offerings were presented to those gathered in the Sanctuary. On that Sunday we had the largest Sunday School attendance for the entire year with twenty extra adults involved. Even if all the new people did not plug into the program, at least they had been properly introduced. Small groups of all sorts would be essential if the church were to maintain its sense of closeness and be able to assimilate new people into the fellowship

❖ **New Member Sunday**

A second New Member Sunday was organized with letters and phone calls to people who had been visiting. Five more people became new members near the end of May. Having people join the church in the midst of an interim appointment is one of the best ways to raise the morale of a congregation. It tells the congregation that people are joining the congregation not simply choosing a church on the basis of the senior pastor.

❖ **Preparing for a New Senior Pastor**

Efforts to pave the way for the new senior pastor began with the announcement of her coming in March. She met with the Staff Parish Relations Committee and they began a word of mouth promotion of her. In addition, she was invited to meet with the entire staff, with individual staff members, the associate, and with me as interim pastor. Plans for a pictorial directory were launched as an essential tool for her learning the names of church members.

Since the Transformation program had already been approved and meetings planned in April and May, I asked that she attend those meetings in my place so she could be on board when she came in July. I worked with the SPRC on various ways she and her family could be welcomed to the church and community. I also dedicated one sermon

Second Interim

and one reflection to the issue of the role of ministers and their needs as people. I hoped the church would become more conscientious about their responsibility to nurture the new pastoral family rather than simply waiting to make a quick assessment of the pastor's acceptability as their new leader.

PREACHING PLAN

Following the Lenten series on the Sermon of the Mount, I preached a variety of sermons trying to cover both personal and church life. Listed below are several of the sermons with brief description of their themes.

> *Rat Race Retirement!* Isaiah 55:1-3a; 1Corinthians 9:24-27

This sermon addressed the need to find ways of dealing with stress, ways of finding *peace within the pace*. Worship, meditation, and the pursuit of love and caring were ways of beginning the journey toward wholeness.

> *Time to Tangibilitate!* Matthew 6:19-21

This stewardship sermon dealt with how we should offer our "tangible" gifts to God. I shared with the congregation my own stewardship journey and invited them to learn to give out of gratitude to God.

> *Eat, Drink and Remember* 1 Corinthians 11:23-25

In the worship survey results, the church ranked communion as one of the most important elements of worship. This sermon endeavored to share a theology of this sacrament and to explain that central to its meaning was "remembering" the Christ—remembering his life, death, resurrection, and life-giving teaching.

> *How to Treat Your Minister* John 1:6-9

In the text from John, we find these words: "There was a man, sent from God, who name was John." Based on these words I suggested that, like John, ministers are human (man), divinely called (sent from God), and each unique (whose name was John). I encouraged members to remember and honor each of these aspects as they sought to minister to their spiritual shepherd.

PASTORAL REFLECTIONS

Listed below are summaries of the reflections written from Easter until the end of May.

➢ *The Grace of God in our Hands*

This reflection spoke of the importance of doing "hands on" ministry and invited the congregation to join with me in a mission project called "Amigos Days" where volunteers repair homes of those unable to do so themselves.

➢ *Why I'm Big on Small Groups*

As part of an invitation to be a part of a Sunday School promotional event, I shared my theology of small groups and why it is important for developing community and enriching one's faith.

➢ *When the Shepherd is Feeling Sheepish*

This reflection was a simple reminder that the shepherd of the church will need shepherding and nurturing, just as members need the same. I invited the congregation to take responsibility to welcome, nurture, and support the new senior pastor.

➤ *Forgetting What Lies Behind!*

My first sermon was based on the text from Philippians where Paul urges us to forget what lies behind. I urged the congregation to do just that as they sought to grow as a church. Preoccupation with the past will cripple the church and prevent it from being a vital and growing church.

➤ *Looking Backward; Looking Forward!*

In this piece I looked back over my time at the church and celebrated the victories. I thanked the congregation for its love and support of me during my tenure there. I expressed my confidence in their future and asked for God's continual blessing on their life and work. (The complete text of this reflection appears at the end of this section.)

STATE OF THE CHURCH

As I left the church, I was pleased that it had recovered so remarkably since my first visit in December. Morale was good. Attendance was much improved. Giving had progressed from an average of $9,500 a Sunday to $12,000 a Sunday (Still below where it needed to be, but close to budget needs). Youth and children's ministries made improvement despite having lost two staff members responsible for those programs. The church was poised to make the transition to a new senior pastor without a major controversy or divisiveness. I left knowing that the church was truly ready for new leadership and eager to become a vital church again.

Challenges Ahead

Even though I left the church in a much improved state, it had many challenges ahead of it. Central to its future was redefining its vision. Care needed to be taken to clarify whether that vision included some notion of size. Care also was needed so that future growth would not endanger one of its key strengths—"a diverse and caring community of faith." If steps were not taken to ensure community building through small groups then that sense of family might be lost. Indeed, I thought small groups should be one of the major emphases of the church's programming.

The building of the stewardship support of the church is also crucial to its future. More money is needed to start paying down the debt on the building. More money is needed to fund the expansion of staff—perhaps in the areas of children and youth. This growth in stewardship can come in part from increased giving of present members but it will also need to be reinforced by an influx of new members. New member recruitment is a must for the years ahead.

A church, like people, needs time to recover after a trauma. This resilient church had been through an emotional and traumatic time. It did not need new controversy but rather a new spirit of fellowship, forgiveness and love. Worship, fellowship, and spiritual renewal could help prepare for a brighter tomorrow. I left with high expectations for this church being a vital, caring, missional community of faith. It was already well on its way!

❖ **Saying Goodbye** (Final Reflection)

Second Interim

Looking Backward, Looking Forward

Carol Burnett sang it almost every time she performed. I'll say it only once—but really mean it—"I'm so glad we had this time together." These past five months have passed so quickly, the last few even faster that the first. So much has happened since I simultaneously began this job and Medicare and celebrated a birthday! Morale has changed. Giving has changed. Energy in worship has changed. Confidence in the future has changed. (And all for the better, I might add.) I'm glad to have been a part of that dramatic recovery. I have been very intentional in my leadership. I have given you my best. But it is you who have made the difference. It is you who have decided to believe in yourself, each other, and in your church's future. I applaud you for your resilience.

Looking back I see great improvement. Looking forward I see great potential. You are now ready to really make great strides as a church. You are poised to set a new vision for the church and move boldly toward that vision. You have a great staff, a great new senior pastor on her way, and outstanding lay leadership in place. What more do you need?

You need, I believe, a new level of commitment from every member—a commitment to be active, to attend worship regularly, to grow through study and mission, to put back into the church some of the blessing you have received from the church. Please remember that summer is no time to take a vacation from the church but rather a time to worship as a vital rhythm of your life.

July will mark the beginning role of your new senior minister. I trust you will be ready to welcome her and her family. Welcome them *warmly*. (It will be July, after all!) I also hope some of you will be willing to be more to them than just parishioners, that you will also be people they can trust, people they can call friends. Take it from a minister of 39 years, without such closeness, ministry can be a very lonely profession.

As I leave this congregation, I do not say goodbye as I hope to see many of you again. I plan to keep track of your ministry as you forge boldly into the future. I have great hopes—no, make that "great expectations"—for who you will become as a church.

May God continue to bless you as individuals and as a community of faith!

With love and affection, Pastor Justin

Interim Ministry

EPILOGUE: HEALTH OF CHURCHES AFTER INTERIM

I am pleased to report that during the years since my two interim appointments, both churches have done remarkably well especially considering the challenges they have faced. Both made smooth transitions with the coming of the new pastor. Both have made great strides in becoming financially stable having each completed a successful debt-retirement program. Both remain committed to mission as a major expression of their church identity. Both could be strong arguments for the effectiveness of interim ministry as a means of making positive changes in the midst of critical and difficult times.

Recently I have visited both churches and found the morale to be energized, upbeat, and welcoming. It is hard to imagine that these are the same two churches I first experienced in deep grief and devastating frustration. I am most proud of the resiliency of these two churches. I served them both only briefly but during that time I was privileged to witness incredible strides towards becoming the church God had called them to be. I am hopeful that others will find in interim ministry what I have found—an incredible opportunity to bring a word of guidance, hope and challenge to churches in the midst of transition.

Interim Ministry

REFLECTIONS ON INTERIM MINISTRY

General Observations

❖ One Crisis Calls for Another

I am now convinced that there are no *"one issue"* interims. True, one obvious issue may be in the forefront (like the grieving process at the loss of a pastor, or a financial crisis, or a conflict between members of the church), but where there is one issue brewing, others will likely erupt. The interim pastor must be able to detect new issues that need to be addressed and never be content with simply dealing with the obvious ones at the onset.

❖ Take the Hit! Bite the Bullet!

If there are any issues that have the potential for negative fallout, the interim pastor should be willing to risk taking on the problem. If the interim minister can "take the fall" thus sparing that role for the next pastor, then it is the responsible and prudent thing do. Once the interim pastor has *taken the hit,* he or she can simply forgive the aggressors and move on, perhaps never having to face that person or those persons ever again. The new pastor can thereby avoid an early conflict and all the accompanying collateral damage. When the interim pastor experiences harsh criticism as a result of tackling a tough issue, such a consequence is not senseless suffering but one done for the sake of the church and for the well-being of the next pastor.

❖ Theological and Personal Maturity Required

Since one of the roles of the interim pastor may be to pay the price for tough decisions, then emotional maturity is most certainly required. Seasoned wisdom and a wealth of experience in life and in the church can also come in handy. In volatile times of transition, it is crucial that the interim pastor have adequate self-esteem and a well-grounded theological perspective. Interim clergy should expect certain negative fallout in a time of crisis, some, rightly or wrongly, directed solely at the interim pastor. There are several helpful mantras for those times: "Don't take it personally!" "It is not about you, stupid." The interim experience is no time for "finding oneself" or formulating a theology of the church or developing a methodology for crisis management. It is a time of knowing oneself, already understanding the church's ministry and being able to act decisively within the context of both.

❖ Preach the Word!

No ministerial function is more important during interim ministry than preaching the word. In doing so, great care should be taken to avoid using old sermons or blindly following the lectionary with no regard to the present situation. What is required is *tailor-made preaching*, much in the style of the apostle Paul who applied the emerging biblical faith to concrete issues in the life of the church. It is the inescapable responsibility of the interim pastor to bring a biblical and theological word to the issues being faced by the congregation and to do so believing that such faith, when coupled with the Holy Spirit, will be sufficient for the day. Grace will be equal to every need;

dead bones can come to life; the spirit of forgiveness can overcome an atmosphere of contentiousness. The interim pastor must be able to discern what word the congregation needs to hear and when it should be proclaimed. Careful sermon planning as well as effective execution must be the order of the day.

- ❖ **Love the People!**

The interim pastor is never simply a problem solver or a change agent. There is one essential action required as the pastor enters a crisis interim situation—love the people. There is no substitute for that essential act and no amount of leadership finesse or ministerial skill will make up for its absence. I am not talking about being warm and fuzzy but rather caring, empathetic and insightful. Even genuine love must be combined with wisdom, forethought and shrewdness to serve the church effectively. Every act of ministry will be greatly enhanced if the interim minister expresses a true love for the people.

- ❖ **Interim, Not Limbo!**

The interim time is not one of limbo or marking time but one that is actively monitoring and enabling a healthy transition. Significant changes should not be reserved for the new pastor who will follow but rather inaugurated by the interim pastor. Indeed, a time of crisis is one ripe for change and nothing should prevent that change from being immediate and largely positive. When the interim time period works as it should, many positive changes will have taken place. In such cases the laity will be able to say as they welcome the new pastor, "So much progress has already been made; we can't wait for you to continue to lead us to greater ministry and service."

ROLE OF PREACHING IN INTERIM MINISTRY

❖ **Honor the Importance of Preaching**

Preaching is the most important task for the interim minister. Its role is to be the interpreter of both the biblical faith and the current culture. In times of crisis, interim preaching is called to offer insights into the situation at hand and to give a theology of hope for the future. Preaching will often be the most powerful tool in addressing such issues as grief, despair, disillusionment, anger, forgiveness, and conflict.

❖ **Preach Only Tailor-made Sermons**

The interim is not a time to pull out old sermons or blindly follow the lectionary. In addressing the issues, the preacher may draw from the entire Bible to find the appropriate text or texts. The lectionary should be the starting point but not the mandatory rule. Careful planning should ensure that important aspects of the faith be preached during this time of transition.

❖ **Preach First to the Situation at Hand**

The first sermon preached in the interim should address any key issues or problems in the church. These may be dynamics of grief, responding to clerical misconduct, conflict within the church, issues of racism or injustice. Just as Paul wrote letters that addressed specific issues or problems in the church, so should the interim preacher address issues that are immediately apparent. Failure to acknowledge the "elephant in the room" will only cause more anxiety on the part of the congregation. Even so, one should never assume that there is only one issue to be addressed no matter how dominant that issue is. For example, after the death of a beloved and charismatic pastor, the issue at hand may not only be grief but also a confusion of church identity in the face of that loss.

❖ **Discern When to Leave the Issue(s) at Hand**

As important as detecting and dealing with critical issues in the church, equally important is knowing when to more on. Preaching in the interim should address systemic issues of the church as well as personal needs of individual members. A church in grief may need four sermons that deal in different ways with grief and the aspect of hope, but it does not need four months of such a diet. To heal, people need to focus on other aspects of the gospel and of the Christian life. A church in grief needs to be given permission to laugh again.

❖ **Always Preach Hope**

From the first meeting to the first sermon, the minister should exhibit the spirit of hope. Even when a situation is extremely tragic, even when church members are in total despair, the interim minister must always believe in hope and be able to preach that the power of God is sufficient in the face of all circumstances.

❖ **Include the Formative Tasks in Preaching**

Preaching during an interim appointment is often in the midst of change and crisis—a great time to wrestle with formative issues (history, identity, direction, leadership, and connection.) Subject matter may include such topics as the mission of the church, the vision of a congregation, the connection with the larger church, the role of stewardship, how a congregation should treat the pastor, and worship identity.

❖ Use Other Forms of Communication to Enhance Preaching

When complex issues are being addressed, using various forms of church communication—church newsletter, discussion forums, letters to the congregation—can set the stage for the preached word. Indeed, some discussion and dissemination of information can best be done through the printed page. When used in tandem—the printed word and the spoken word—both will be enriched. For example, when ideas are first shared in a pastoral reflection and then followed by a thought-provoking sermon, the effectiveness of the sermon is greatly increased and the pastoral reflection becomes firmly grounded in the biblical faith.

❖ Plan Carefully the Worship Context

During the interim appointment the preacher should begin by using familiar worship practices when possible. Continuity in worship is often helpful, but especially so if the church is in crisis. As in all worship planning, care should be taken that the service move smoothly and have a unifying theme thus strengthening the effectiveness of the sermon and deepening the total worship experience.

❖ Use Listening and Pastoral Care to Strengthen the Preached Word

The more pastoral care the interim minister can do, the more informed the preaching can be. In addition, the personal contact will make the congregation feel more connected to the pastor as they listen from the pew. If the pastor listens to them, they are more likely to return the favor. Listening, in fact, is one of the most important preparations one can do for preaching. Without it one might be able to interpret the word but be inadequately prepared to apply it to the specific needs of the congregation. Preaching without much personal contact runs the risk of "missing the mark" on Sunday.

❖ Be Oneself

Using one's unique gifts, graces, and style in the act of preaching is important in interim ministry as it underscores the variety of personalities and abilities of each minister. Though the minister should honor when possible local worship traditions, one should not be forced to "give up the sling shot in favor of Saul's armor." For example, one might refuse to use film clips as a regular tool in preaching the contemporary service if that did not mesh with one's style of preaching. However, jettisoning the robe and stole for a dressy polo shirt and slacks might be an appropriate concession—a compromise that would not affect one's preaching.

❖ Preach with Humility

The more dramatically one preaches, the greater the temptation to draw attention to oneself instead of the message, and to think that the positive responses are mainly a result of one's own skills. But the ultimate effectiveness of preaching rests in the workings of the Holy Spirit and in the minds and hearts of willing listeners. The preacher must do his or her part in preparation and then trust the results to God.

KEYS TO EFFECTIVE INTERIM MINISTRY

- ✓ Study carefully the church's history and tradition.
- ✓ Set personal and church goals at the beginning of interim.
- ✓ Diagnose the problems and issues the church is facing.
- ✓ Re-present the biblical faith in word, action, and spirit.
- ✓ Offer a less-anxious presence.
- ✓ Listen to the people with heart and mind.
- ✓ Analyze critically all feedback.
- ✓ Share your observations and insights about the church with the congregation.
- ✓ Interact with the congregation in a variety of settings.
- ✓ Engage in critical pastoral care.
- ✓ Take on any issue or problem that needs addressing; don't leave it for the next pastor.
- ✓ Don't take negative behavior personally; simply expect it and deflect it.
- ✓ Always believe in the people and in the possibility for positive change.
- ✓ Celebrate every victory no matter how small.
- ✓ Never accept full credit for positive results; give credit to other leaders, to God, and to the people.
- ✓ Prepare the way for the one who is coming.
- ✓ Pass the baton smoothly and decisively when your leg of the race is complete.

Made in the USA
Columbia, SC
01 December 2023